MARRIAGE~AS GOD INTENDED IT TO BE!

Reversing the Trends of Today's Society

JETHRO EKUTA

MARRIAGE~AS GOD INTENDED IT TO BE!

Reversing the Trends of Today's Society

ACW Press
Phoenix, Arizona 85013

All Scripture quotations unless otherwise marked are from the New King James Version, Copyright © 1979, 1980, 1982 by Thomas Nelson, Inc., Publishers. Used by permission.

Scriptures marked KJV are taken from the King James Version of the Bible.

Marriage—As God Intended It to Be!
Copyright ©2001 Jethro Ekuta
All rights reserved

Cover design by Walljasper Design
Interior design by Pine Hill Graphics

Packaged by ACW Press
5501 N. 7th Ave., #502,
Phoenix, Arizona 85013
www.acwpress.com

The views expressed or implied in this work do not necessarily reflect those of ACW Press. Ultimate design, content, and editorial accuracy of this work is the responsibility of the author(s).

Publisher's Cataloging-in-Publication
(Provided by Quality Books, Inc.)

Ekuta, Jethro.
    Marriage--as God intended it to be! / by Jethro Ekuta. -- 1st ed.
    p. cm.
    ISBN: 1-892525-42-9

    1. Marriage--Religious aspects--Christianity.
I. Title.

BV835.E38 2001   248.4
                            QBI01-200183

All rights reserved. No part of this book may be reproduced, stored in a retrieval system, or transmitted in any form or by any means–electronic, mechanical, photocopying, recording, or otherwise–without prior permission in writing from the copyright holder except as provided by USA copyright law.

Printed in the United States of America.

To the loving memory of my mother, Florence, from whom I learned, firsthand, the role of a godly wife and a godly mother in the family.

Contents

Preface
Acknowledgments

1. The Marriage Institution: An Overview 17
   The Origin of Marriage 17
   The Purpose of Marriage 20
   Summary 23
   Challenges 23

2. Choosing a Marriage Partner 25
   Who Should a Christian Marry? 25
   God as the Source of the Right Companion 30
   Trusting God for Guidance in Choosing
      the Right Companion 33
   Summary 41
   Challenges 42

3. Courtship 43
   Different Courtship Scenarios 44
   How Long Should Courtship Last? 47
   Can I Engage in Sexual Intercourse with My Partner
      During Courtship? 48
   Things To Do During Courtship 50
   Things Not To Do During Courtship 57
   Summary 59
   Challenges 59

4. The Marriage Ceremony........................ 61
    What To Do When Parents Say "No".................... 62
    The Wedding Ceremony............................. 65
    Summary... 73
    Challenges....................................... 74
5. Administrative Set-up of the Home 75
    Summary... 77
    Challenges....................................... 77
6. Duties of the Man in the Home 79
    Duties of a Man As Leader 80
    Duties of a Man As Husband........................ 85
    Summary... 94
    Challenges....................................... 95
7. Duties of the Woman in the Home 97
    Duties of a Woman As Wife......................... 98
    Some Destructive Attributes of An Ungodly Wife.......... 104
    Crowning Qualities of Womanhood.................... 105
    Temptresses...................................... 110
    Godly Women Married to Ungodly Men................. 113
    Summary... 113
    Challenges....................................... 113
8. Parental Duties 115
    Parental Influence and Examples..................... 125
    Parental Weaknesses and Sins: Indulgence of Children 128
    Summary... 132
    Challenge 132
9. Facts about Children........................... 133
    Children Are Gifts from God........................ 133
    Children Are Esteemed Highly....................... 134
    Exhortations to Children........................... 135
    Special Promises to Children 136
    Ungrateful Children 137

  Examples of Helpful Children 139
  Vices of Children. 140
  Examples of Good Children of Good Parentage 140
  Examples of Good Children of Wicked Men 141
  Different Ways Children Can Dishonor Their Parents. 142
  Summary 143
  Challenge 144

10. Enemies of the Home 145
  Adultery. 145
  Polygamy 147
  Divorce. 151
  Satan 164
  An Unforgiving Spirit. 166
  Television 167
  Friends, Relations, and Other People 168
  Dishonesty 169
  Finances 170
  Career 175
  Lack of, or Ineffective, Communication 175
  Computers 176
  Quarrels. 177
  Summary 179
  Challenges. 179

11. Additional Family Issues. 181
  Family Devotion 181
  Family Planning 182
  Cross-Cultural Marriage. 182
  Sex in Marriage 183
  Driving to Church Together. 184
  Godliness 184
  Summary 185
  Challenges. 185

About the Author

Preface

Many years before I even thought of marriage, God impressed upon my heart that I would be a marriage counselor. I could not understand how God could call a young man to this profession who knew nothing about marriage; nonetheless, I believed God and pondered over this calling in my heart. The only person I told was the woman to whom I am now married. When I met her and became convinced that we would become husband and wife, I shared my calling with her and asked whether she would support me in this endeavor. Fortunately, my wife shared my vision of ministry. My marriage has not been a perfect one, being subject to the same pressures that every marriage goes through. My wife and I have learned to depend on God daily to sustain our marriage. His grace has thus far been sufficient for us. I could not possibly have had a better companion or a better family. Praise be to God for His loving-kindness!

This book is a culmination of several years of teachings on marriage. While a graduate student at the University of Mississippi, my wife and I organized a week-long marriage seminar at the Church of the Living God, Toccopola, Mississippi. This was our first direct involvement in the ministry of marriage counseling to which God had called us many years before. Members of the church were so receptive, we were invited to teach the same material at another Mississippi church.

When we moved to Nashville, Tennessee in 1995, God led my family to join the African Christian Fellowship (later, the Beautiful Gate Church). I became a Sunday school teacher in the church and God impressed upon me to teach a series of lessons on "The Christian Family." These teachings lasted for seven months. During that time, I never knew in advance what I would teach the following Sunday. I depended on God completely for what lessons to teach. Sometimes, I never knew what I would teach until the early hours of the Sunday in which the lesson was to be taught. I made up my mind I would not consult any book ever written on marriage, but rather dig into God's Word and depend on Him for guidance.

God did not fail me, but always gave me the Bible passages to use and the words to say while teaching. During the initial lessons, I had no thought of writing a book on marriage but, as the series progressed, the Lord inspired me to write down the lessons He had taught me and put them into book form. I kept every note I used for the lessons and developed these notes into this book. God also gave me the title of the book. He confirmed the inspiration to write a book through several people: A member of the church suggested that I write and compile a handout of all the lessons I had taught; my wife felt a burden that I should write a book; and my pastor, Dr. Gideon Olaleye, told the congregation he thought I had done a good job and should compile the teachings into a handout. With these suggestions, and God's backing, I set out to write this book. Under God's guidance and help, I have been able to complete the formidable task.

Preface

This book is written for young Christians who aspire to get married, for young Christian couples who do not know what the future holds for their marriage, and for Christian couples who are going through negative experiences in marriage. It can also be used as an evangelical tool for those who do not know the Lord but wish to know Him and see His hand at work in their marriage.

Most marriage books discuss one or a few aspects of marriage in-depth. In my experience, it is hard to find a book in Christian or secular bookstores that covers every major aspect of marriage in a single collection. This book was written to fill that gap and to provide a concise collection in a single edition of Bible passages that speak on all major issues related to marriage. I believe the Holy Spirit is able to teach people once they are exposed to appropriate passages. Consequently, in this book, several passages are cited with little or no further explanation.

In order to ensure that the reader has an opportunity to read every important Bible passage dealing with marriage, the passages cited are reproduced in full, using the New King James Version (unless otherwise stated). In many instances, when passages are merely cited in a book, people rarely open their Bibles to read the verses. In this book, the reader has the opportunity to read every cited passage without having a Bible handy. Each referenced passage is indented and italicized. The reader is encouraged to consult other books that discuss these topics in-depth if a deeper understanding is desired.

The first ten chapters of this book discuss a particular aspect of marriage, whereas chapter eleven deals with additional family issues that do not fit well into any of the other chapters. A summary of the lessons discussed in each chapter is presented at the end of the chapter, followed by a series of questions that challenge the reader to specific actions.

I pray that people contemplating marriage will find the book useful; that those already married will be inspired and encouraged; that those contemplating divorce will reconsider their decision; and that those already divorced will be encouraged.

May God bless you as you read.
Jethro Ekuta

Acknowledgments

I am grateful to Dr. Thomas Clark of Thomas Clark Associates for proofreading and providing many insightful thoughts and suggestions for improving the manuscript; and to Pastors Wayne Lowe and Bob Lowery of Faith Bible Church for proofreading and offering invaluable suggestions for improving the manuscript. I owe much appreciation to Barbara Robidoux of TCC Manuscript Service for professionally editing the manuscript and offering valuable suggestions.

I am also grateful to my wife, Roseline, and our four children for creating the opportunity for the "school of marriage" in which I put the teachings of this book into practice. I am thankful to everyone who has made a major impact on my life.

Above all, I am grateful to God for the inspiration and for making the writing of this book possible.

Jethro Ekuta

1

The Marriage Institution: An Overview

THE ORIGIN OF MARRIAGE

Marriage is an institution established by God. Its very idea was conceived by Him. The origin of marriage can be traced back to the Garden of Eden following God's creation of the first man, Adam. In that first marriage, God was the Officiating Minister. Marriage was instituted when God declared:

> "It is not good that the man should be alone; I will make him a helper comparable to him." (Genesis 2:18)

The Bible does not tell us just how long it was after Adam's creation before God made the woman. What we do know, however, is that Adam was alone—without a woman—for some time. During his period of solitude, Adam apparently knew there was a void in his life and felt the need to fill this void but he did not know how. That he was aware of this helpless situation is implied in the following statement:

> "So Adam gave names to all cattle, to the birds of the air, and to every beast of the field. But for Adam there was not found a helper comparable to him." (Genesis 2:20)

Adam's only companions were the beasts of the field that God had made. He named every one of these beasts but he could not find a companion for himself. Thus, God took the initiative to create a special being that was comparable to him as follows:

> "And the Lord God caused a deep sleep to fall on Adam, and he slept; and He took one of his ribs, and closed up the flesh in its place. Then the rib which the Lord God had taken from man He made into a woman, and He brought her to the man." (Genesis 2:21-22)

The special being that God made was different from all the beasts that Adam knew. Once Adam saw this being, he knew without a shadow of doubt that she would be a helper comparable to him. His satisfaction with the woman (Eve) God provided for him was quite vivid and he remarked concerning her:

The Marriage Institution: An Overview

> *"This is now bone of my bones and flesh of my flesh; she shall be called Woman, because she was taken out of Man."* (Genesis 2:23)

In making the first woman, God performed the first general anesthesia and the first surgery known to mankind.

The rib God took out of Adam to make Eve is significant in many respects:

First, the removal of a rib from Adam created an empty space in his body. That space remained a perpetual void in him until he found the woman. So it is with every man—being a descendant of Adam, he has a void in his flesh—the missing rib—that can only be filled satisfactorily by a woman who is "comparable to him." (Genesis 2:20) It is, therefore, not surprising that men are attracted to women.

Second, ribs are of different shapes and sizes. Replacing the missing "rib" with just any type of rib will not fill the void in a man's life but will rather create pain, agony and misery. Just as donating an organ to a needy person without careful scrutiny to match the donor and recipient could create a graft rejection, a man who fills the void in his life with just any woman who is not a proper match, i.e., not comparable to him, will soon find grounds for incompatibility and eventual rejection. Every man must seek to fill the void in his life with the appropriate "rib" (woman). In other words, a man must seek a woman who is appropriate for him. Not every woman in the world is appropriate for every man and vice versa. Likewise, every woman must seek to fill the empty space in a suitable man. The principles for choosing an appropriate partner will be discussed in the next chapter.

Third, the rib was made into a woman, not into another man. This implies that a man cannot fill the void in his life with another man. Likewise, a woman cannot fill the void in another woman because another woman has no such void to be filled. God has put the void in men and He has created women to fill the void. When there is an appropriate match between a man and a woman, both of them are bound to find fulfillment in their lives. God made the man and the woman to be complementary to each other and He intended marriage to be a relationship between the two.

Finally, the rib is located on the side of the body, thereby denoting intimacy of the man and the woman. And the rib is located close to the heart; therefore, the woman is to be loved and protected by the man and she is to have a special place in his life.

The Purpose of Marriage

God does not do anything without some purpose behind it. When He instituted marriage, He had three purposes in mind.

1. Marriage was instituted for companionship

Companionship was the driving force behind the institution of marriage.

> "And the Lord God said, 'It is not good that the man should be alone; I will make him a helper comparable to him.'" (Genesis 2:20)

A companion is a close friend and one of a pair. A man is lonely until he finds a suitable woman; no parent, sister, brother, or friend can satisfy his desire for true companionship. The author of Ecclesiastes writes:

The Marriage Institution: An Overview

> *"Two are better than one, because they have a good reward for their labor. For if they fall, one will lift up his companion. But woe to him who is alone when he falls, for he has no one to help him up. Again, if two lie down together, they will keep warm; but how can one be warm alone? Though one may be overpowered by another, two can withstand him. And a threefold cord is not quickly broken."* (4:9-12)

In this passage, companionship increases wealth because two people have a "good reward for their labor." Companionship also provides strength, encouragement, and comfort during moments of distress and depression because "if they fall, one will lift up his companion." Furthermore, companionship creates warmth—"if two lie down together, they will keep warm." Finally, companionship brings about unity which, in turn, has a positive force for "though one may be overpowered by another, two can withstand him. And a threefold cord is not quickly broken."

2. Marriage was instituted for procreation

It is the will of God that a marriage be fruitful through procreation.

> *"So God created man in His own image; in the image of God He created him; male and female He created them. Then God said to them, Be fruitful and multiply; fill the earth and subdue it; have dominion over the fish of the sea, over the birds of the air, and over every living thing that moves on the earth."* (Genesis 1:27-28)

When God created Adam and Eve, He equipped them with the ability to reproduce. In fact, He commanded them to do so. Children are esteemed highly by God; they are special to Him. One of the greatest miracles the world sees every day is that of reproduction, spanning the period from conception to delivery. God intended that children be born into this world through marriage—and only through marriage! The following passage supports that assertion and reveals the mind of God concerning the seriousness of marriage:

> "She is your companion and your wife by covenant. But did He not make them one...? And why one? He seeks godly offspring. Therefore take heed to your spirit and let none deal treacherously with the wife of his youth." (Malachi 2:14-15)

Godly offspring come out of a marriage. God is constantly seeking godly offspring from among married couples.

3. Marriage was instituted for sexual intercourse

Sex is not dirty and it is not sinful when carried out within the bounds of a legitimate marriage. Sex is a gift from God and He meant it for the good of human beings, although it is increasingly misused and perverted.

> "Nevertheless, because of sexual immorality, let each man have his own wife, and let each woman have her own husband. Let the husband render to his wife the affection due her, and likewise also the wife to her husband. The wife does not have authority over her own body, but the husband does. And likewise the husband does not have authority over his own body, but the wife does. Do not deprive one another except with consent for a time, that you may give yourselves to fasting and prayer; and come

The Marriage Institution: An Overview

together again so that Satan does not tempt you because of your lack of self-control." (I Corinthians 7:2-5)

God created human sexuality but He instructed humankind in the acceptable way that sexual desires are to be satisfied. Sexual intercourse outside marriage is considered immoral by God. Sexual intercourse by an unmarried person is termed fornication. If a married person engages in sexual intercourse with anyone other than his or her spouse, such a relationship constitutes an act of adultery. Adultery and fornication are both considered serious acts of immorality by God and they carry grave consequences. This subject will be dealt with in greater detail in subsequent chapters. It suffices to say that,

"Marriage is honorable among all, and the bed undefiled; but fornicators and adulterers God will judge." (Hebrews 13:4)

Summary

1. God instituted marriage.
2. The purpose of marriage is for companionship, procreation, and sexual intimacy.

Challenges

1. What are your views on the origin and purpose of marriage?
2. How are your views on marriage different from God's views as revealed in the Bible?
3. What would you do to reconcile your views with God's views, if different?

2

Choosing a Marriage Partner

Who Should a Christian Marry?

As noted in the previous chapter, God instituted marriage. He also established the principles of a successful marriage. Marriage is like a game, and failure to play this game by God's rules, or an attempt to play it by a set of rules established by man, is bound to result in frustration and the ultimate demise of the marriage.

A successful marriage begins with the choice of the appropriate "rib" (i.e., companion). Through His Word, God has provided humanity with guidance on how to choose a partner. The first consideration is to identify the pool of people from which to choose. Before we consider this pool, let us first consider the pool from which Christians are not to choose a partner. For Christians, the entire world does not constitute the pool from which to choose a partner. A believer, i.e., someone who has accepted Jesus Christ as his or her personal Savior and Lord, must not marry an unbeliever. Let us examine some of God's instructions to His children through the ages.

In searching for a wife for his son, Isaac, Abraham instructed his servant:

> *"Put your hand under my thigh, and I will make you swear by the Lord, the God of heaven and the God of the earth, that you will not take a wife for my son from the daughters of the Canaanites, among whom I dwell; but you shall go to my country and to my kindred, and take a wife for my son Isaac."* (Genesis 24:2-4)

The Canaanites were idol worshippers; therefore, they did not know the God of Abraham. Abraham and his ancestors were idol worshippers until God called him from among his people and set him apart for His use. The patriarch heeded God's voice, left his country and its idol worship practices, and became loyal to God alone as he sojourned in a foreign land, the land of Canaan. Since Abraham dwelt among the Canaanites, he was troubled that his son might become a husband to one of the Canaanite maids. He knew such a union between the godly and the ungodly would destroy the godly.

It is obvious, that before he died, Abraham instructed Isaac concerning the need to dissuade his children from marrying the Canaanites. Apparently, Isaac heeded Abraham's admonition.

> "Then Isaac called Jacob and said to him: You shall not take a wife from the daughters of Canaan. Arise, go to Padan Aram, to the house of Bethuel your mother's father; and take yourself a wife from there of the daughters of Laban your mother's brother." (Genesis 28:1-2)

After the deliverance of the children of Israel from their bondage in Egypt, Moses gave them the following instruction which he had received from God:

> "When the Lord your God brings you into the land which you go to possess, and has cast out many nations before you, the Hittites and the Girgashites and the Amorites and the Canaanites and the Perizzites and the Hivites and the Jebusites, seven nations greater and mightier than you, and the Lord your God delivers them over to you, you shall conquer them and utterly destroy them. You shall make no covenant with them nor show mercy to them. Nor shall you make marriages with them. You shall not give your daughter to their son, nor take their daughter for your son. For they will turn your sons away from following me, to serve other gods; so the anger of the Lord will be aroused against you and destroy you suddenly." (Deuteronomy 7:1-4)

This passage explains clearly the reason for God's disapproval of a marriage union between a godly and an ungodly person. It is His will to preserve His children from pollution from the world around them.

Joshua, exhorting the children of Israel in his last days, cautioned them against ungodly marriage unions.

> "Therefore, take diligent heed to yourselves, that you love the Lord your God. Or else, if indeed you do go back and cling to the remnant of these nations—these that remain among you—and make marriages with them, and go in to them and they to you, know for certain that the Lord your God will no longer drive out these nations from before you. But they shall be snares and traps to you, and scourges on your sides and thorns in your eyes, until you perish from this good land which the Lord your God has given you." (Joshua 23:11-13)

Ezra, while confessing the sins of the children of Israel, recalled God's indignation over marriage unions between His people and the ungodly.

> "And now, O our God, what shall we say after this? For we have forsaken Your commandments, which You commanded by Your servants the prophets, saying, The land which you are entering to possess is an unclean land, with the uncleanness of the peoples of the lands, with their abominations which have filled it from one end to another with their impurity. Now therefore, do not give your daughters as wives for their sons, nor take their daughters to your sons; and never seek their peace or prosperity, that you may be strong and eat the good of the land, and leave it as an inheritance to your children forever. And after all that has come upon us for our evil deeds and for our great guilt, since You our God have punished us less than our iniquities deserve, and have given us such deliverance as this, should we again break Your commandments, and join in marriage with the people of these abominations? Would you not be angry with

us until You had consumed us, so that there would be no remnant or survivor?" (Ezra 9:10-14)

In his reforms at Jerusalem, Nehemiah expressed disgust over the intermarriage between the children of Israel and the heathen around them.

"In those days I also saw the Jews who had married women of Ashdod, Ammon, and Moab. And half of their children spoke the language of Ashdod, and could not speak the language of Judah, but spoke according to the language of one or the other people. So I contended with them and cursed them, struck some of them and pulled out their hair, and made them swear by God, saying, 'You shall not give your daughters as wives to their sons, nor take their daughters for your sons or yourselves. Did not Solomon king of Israel sin by these things? Yet among many nations there was no king like him, who was beloved of his God; and God made him king over all Israel. Nevertheless pagan women caused even him to sin. Should we then hear of your doing all this great evil, transgressing against our God by marrying pagan women?'" (Nehemiah 13:23-27)

Some skeptics may be living under the false impression that God's injunction of godly people not marrying ungodly people was directed at the children of Israel but not to present-day Christians. However, Paul warns:

"Do not be unequally yoked together with unbelievers. For what fellowship has righteousness with lawlessness? And what communion has light with darkness? And what

> accord has Christ with Belial? Or what part has a believer with an unbeliever? And what agreement has the temple of God with idols? For you are the temple of the living God..." (II Corinthians 6:14-18)

It is thus apparent that God expects a believer to marry only a believer—the pool of people from which a Christian should choose a partner.

God as the Source of the Right Companion

Now that we have established the scriptural basis that believers should marry believers, let us examine why God is the source of the right companion, followed by an outline of the steps involved in choosing a marriage partner. In most cultures, the man initiates the process of seeking a wife, in others, the woman seeks a husband. Nonetheless, God's instructions are applicable to any culture and are capable of guiding us in making life's decisions, including the choice of a marriage partner. The believer can rest assured that God always gives the best mate to His people, if they let Him, and it is important that he or she allows God to choose this partner because:

1. God instituted marriage

God knows the two people who, when joined together in marriage, will best accomplish the purpose of marriage, as outlined in the previous chapter.

2. God is the Master Builder of the home

> "Unless the Lord builds the house, they labor in vain who build it; Unless the Lord guards the city, the watchman stays awake in vain." (Psalm 127:1)

3. A good house must have a solid foundation

Like a rock which makes a solid foundation for a *house,* God is the solid foundation of the *home.* The storms of life will not crush a marriage in which God is the foundation. Therefore, any marriage that is founded upon God will survive any crisis.

> *"Therefore whoever hears these sayings of Mine, and does them, I will liken him to a wise man who built his house on the rock; and the rain descended, the floods came, and the winds blew and beat on that house; and it did not fall, for it was founded on the rock."* (Matthew 7:24-25)

4. God Himself is the source of a prudent partner

Examine each of the following passages.

> *"Houses and riches are an inheritance from fathers, But a prudent wife is from the Lord."* (Proverbs 19:14)

> *"He who finds a wife finds a good thing, And obtains favor from the Lord."* (Proverbs 18:22)

> *"Every good gift and every perfect gift is from above, and comes down from the Father of lights, with whom there is no variation, or shadow of turning."* (James 1:17)

5. God always has man's best interests at heart

> *"For I know the thoughts that I think toward you, says the Lord, thoughts of peace and not of evil, to give you a future and a hope."* (Jeremiah 29:11)

6. Man's methods of choosing are at best faulty

Samuel, one of the greatest Old Testament prophets, erred in his initial attempts to choose King Saul's successor until God cautioned him.

> "So it was, when they came, that he [Samuel] looked at Eliab [Jesse's oldest son] and said, 'Surely the Lord's anointed is before Him!' But the Lord said to Samuel, 'Do not look at his appearance or at the height of his stature, because I have refused him. For the Lord does not see as man sees; for man looks at the outward appearance, but the Lord looks at the heart.'" (I Samuel 16:6-7)

7. God's plans are always better than man's best plans

> "For my thoughts are not your thoughts, nor are your ways my ways, says the Lord. For as the heavens are higher than the earth, so are My ways higher than your ways, and My thoughts than your thoughts." (Isaiah 55:8-9)

The first thing that attracts most men to a woman is her looks. God's infallible word, the Bible, cautions, however, that:

> "Charm is deceitful and beauty is vain, but a woman who fears the Lord, she shall be praised." (Proverbs 31:30)

Inner beauty is always better than outward beauty and God always looks at inner beauty. Peter writes:

> "Do not let your beauty be that outward adorning of arranging the hair, of wearing gold, or of putting on fine

apparel: but let it be the hidden person of the heart, with the incorruptible ornament of a gentle and quiet spirit, which is very precious in the sight of God." (I Peter 3:3-4)

TRUSTING GOD FOR GUIDANCE IN CHOOSING THE RIGHT COMPANION

You can stand upon the promises of God, i.e., claim His promises of providing you with the best spouse that is comparable to you. However, His promises are conditional and are meant only for those who belong to Him. God cannot choose a partner for you if you have no relationship with Him. Therefore, do the first thing first, then you can legitimately stand on His promises. Since marriage is for this life only, it is not worth putting it ahead of our relationship with God. There is no marriage after death. In response to the quest of the Sadducees concerning marriage after death, Jesus answered,

"You are mistaken, not knowing the Scriptures nor the power of God. For in the resurrection they neither marry nor are given in marriage, but are like angels of God in heaven." (Matthew 22:29-30)

If you are not His child, you can become His today as you read this book by taking the following simple steps:

1. **Acknowledge that you are a sinner**
   "For all have sinned and fall short of the glory of God." (Romans 3:23)

2. **Confess your sins to God**
   "If we say that we have no sin, we deceive ourselves, and the truth is not in us. If we confess our sins, He [God] is

faithful and just to forgive us our sins, and to cleanse us from all unrighteousness. If we say that we have not sinned, we make Him a liar, and His word is not in us." (I John 1:8-10)

3. Believe on Jesus Christ and accept Him as your Lord and Savior

"For God so loved the world that He gave His only begotten Son, that whoever believes in Him should not perish but have everlasting life." (John 3:16)

"Behold, I stand at the door and knock. If anyone hears my voice and opens the door, I will come in to him and dine with him, and he with Me." (Revelation 3:20)

"That if you confess with your mouth the Lord Jesus and believe in your heart that God has raised Him from the dead, you will be saved. For with the heart one believes to righteousness, and with the mouth confession is made to salvation." (Romans 10:9-10)

"For by grace you have been saved through faith, and that not of yourselves; it is the gift of God, not of works, lest any man should boast." (Ephesians 2:8-9)

If you have sincerely taken the simple steps outlined above, you are now a child of God. You need to make a commitment to follow Him all the days of your life and strive to please Him daily by living in obedience to His Word, the Bible. As God's child you can claim and stand upon the following promises of God as they pertain to making choices.

1. God will provide the best partner for you

If you make God preeminent in your life, you can be sure that He will provide for you the best partner.

> "But seek first the kingdom of God and His righteousness, and all these things shall be added to you." (Matthew 6:33)

> "Who is the man that fears the Lord? Him shall He teach in the way He chooses." (Psalm 25:12)

2. God will supply you with wisdom

You need wisdom in your search for a companion comparable to you. God is the Source of true wisdom.

> "The fear of the Lord is the beginning of wisdom; A good understanding have all those who do His commandments. His praise endures for ever." (Psalm 111:10)

3. God will give you the desires of your heart

If you delight in the Lord, He will establish your plans.

> "Delight yourself also in the Lord, and He shall give you the desires of your heart. Commit your way to the Lord, Trust also in Him, and He shall bring it to pass." (Psalm 37:4-5)

> "Ask, and it shall be given to you; seek, and you will find; knock, and it will be opened to you: For every one who asks receives, and he who seeks finds, and to him who knocks it will be opened. Or what man is there among you who, if his son asks for bread, will give him a stone? Or if he asks for a fish, will he give him a serpent? If you then,

> being evil, know how to give good gifts to your children, how much more will your Father who is in heaven give good things to those who ask him!" (Matthew 7:7-11)

A major reason we ask and do not receive is because we ask outside His will.

> "You ask and do not receive, because you ask amiss, that you may spend it on your pleasures." (James 4:3)

4. God will direct you to the right partner

> "Trust in the Lord with all your heart, and lean not on your own understanding; In all your ways acknowledge Him, and He shall direct your paths. Do not be wise in your own eyes; Fear the Lord and depart from evil." (Proverbs 3:5-7)

> "The steps of a good man are ordered by the Lord, and He delights in his way." (Psalm 37:23)

5. God will not withhold any good thing from you

> "For the Lord God is a sun and shield; The Lord will give grace and glory; No good thing will he withhold from those who walk uprightly." (Psalm 84:11)

STEPS IN CHOOSING A MARRIAGE PARTNER: A CASE STUDY

Now that we have established the basis for involving God in our choice of a partner, let us examine the steps involved in choosing a partner. For a case study, we will consider in-depth the steps involved in the marriage of Isaac and Rebekah as outlined in Genesis 49.

1. **Be convinced that the time is right for you to get married**
    "To everything there is a season, A time for every purpose under heaven." (Ecclesiastes 3:1)

Is a thirteen-year-old physically, emotionally, and financially mature to assume the responsibilities of marriage? When we know the duties of husbands and wives (discussed in later chapters), the right time for a man or a woman to choose a partner will be self-evident. For Isaac, the right time finally came in Abraham's old age.

2. **If you are a believer, exclude unbelievers from your pool of potential partners.**
    Do not attempt to justify marrying an unbeliever for any reason. Be determined to marry only a believer. Abraham was determined that his son, Isaac, would not marry a person who did not know his God.

> *"So Abraham said to the oldest servant of his house…'Put your hand under my thigh, and I will make you swear by the Lord, the God of heaven and the God of the earth, that you will not take a wife for my son from the daughters of the Canaanites, among whom I dwell; but you shall go to my country and to my kindred, and take a wife for my son Isaac.'"* (Genesis 24:2-4)

3. **Stand on the promises of God concerning His guidance in leading you to the right partner**
    Abraham said,

> *"The Lord God of heaven, who took me from my father's house and from the land of my kindred, and who spoke to*

me and swore unto me, saying, 'To your descendants I give this land, He will send His angel before you, and you shall take a wife for my son from there.'" (Genesis 24:7)

4. Pray that God will reveal to you the partner He has appointed for you

God has appointed a partner for each of His children and He will use daily circumstances of life to bring these two people together. This may include attending the same school, church or other functions simultaneously or simply being in a particular place at a particular time. Abraham's servant prayed that God would reveal Isaac's wife to him in a specific way:

> "Then he [Abraham's servant] said, O Lord God of my master Abraham, please give me success this day, and show kindness to my master Abraham. Behold, I stand here by the well of water, and the daughters of the men of the city are coming out to draw water. Now let it be that the young woman to whom I say, 'Please let down your pitcher that I may drink,' and she says, 'Drink, and I will also give your camels a drink'—let her be the one that You have appointed for your servant Isaac. And by this I will know that you have shown kindness to my master." (Genesis 24:12-14)

5. Expect an answer to your prayer by being watchful

After Abraham's servant had prayed, he waited for expected answer—and the Lord answered him!

> "And it happened, before he had finished speaking, that behold, Rebekah, who was born to Bethuel, son of Milcah, the wife of Nahor, Abraham's brother, came out with her

pitcher on her shoulder. Now the young woman was very beautiful to behold, a virgin; no man had known her. And she went down to the well, filled her pitcher, and came up. And the servant ran to meet her and said, 'Please let me drink a little water from your pitcher.' So she said, 'Drink, my lord.' Then she quickly let her pitcher down to her hand, and gave him a drink. And when she had finished giving him a drink, she said, 'I will draw water for your camels also, until they have finished drinking.' Then she quickly emptied her pitcher into the trough, ran back to the well to draw water, and drew for all his camels. And the man, wondering at her, remained silent so as to know whether the Lord had made his journey prosperous or not." (Genesis 24:15-21)

6. Make the move to approach your partner

If you are convinced that God is leading you to a potential partner, make the move to approach this person and present your request. Abraham's servant made the ultimate move to Rebekah.

> *"[He] said, 'Whose daughter are you? Tell me, please, is there room in your father's house for us to lodge?' So she said to him, 'I am the daughter of Bethuel, Milcah's son, whom she bore to Nahor.' Moreover she said to him, 'We have both straw and feed enough, and room to lodge.'"* (Genesis 24:23-25)

7. Glorify God

If your move is successful, i.e., the potential partner appears to be convinced of a marriage relationship, remember to give all the glory to God. Abraham's servant did.

> "Then the man bowed down his head and worshiped the Lord. And he said, 'Blessed be the Lord God of my master Abraham, who has not forsaken His mercy and His truth toward my master. As for me, being on the way, the Lord led me to the house of my master's brethren.'" (Genesis 24:26-27)

If the potential partner refuses to accept your marriage proposal, reevaluate the steps outlined above to see if you missed something important. Please, be aware that the discussion about Abraham's servant and Rebekah presented above was for illustration of the principles only.

There is no magic recipe for choosing a marriage partner. Therefore, you should not expect things to happen in your own case in the exact same manner as they did for Isaac and Rebekah. Your situation is unique, and God will guide you in a way that is unique to you and your situation; however, the principles are the same.

8. Seek parental consent

Make your decision formal by informing your partner's parents and seeking their consent and blessings. If the relationship is approved by God, He will convince both sets of parents to accept the union as God's will. This happened in the case of Abraham's servant.

> "And I bowed my head and worshiped the Lord, and blessed the Lord God of my master Abraham, who had led me in the way of truth to take the daughter of my master's brother for his son. 'Now if you will deal kindly and truly with my master, tell me. And if not, tell me, that I may turn

to the right hand or to the left.' Then Laban and Bethuel answered and said, 'The thing comes from the Lord; we cannot speak to you either bad or good. Here is Rebekah before you; take her and go, and let her be your master's son's wife, as the Lord has spoken.'" (Genesis 24:48-51)

9. Present gifts to your partner's parents

Following parental consent, a gift should be presented to the family as a token of your love for their child—if your culture accommodates it. That was what Abraham's servant did:

> *"Then the servant brought out jewelry of silver, jewelry of gold, and clothing, and gave them to Rebekah. He also gave precious things to her brother and to her mother."* (Genesis 24:53)

10. Plan for a wedding

Arrange for a wedding. Abraham's servant did (Genesis 24:54-67). Details about the wedding are presented in the next chapter.

SUMMARY

1. It is God's will that a Christian marries only a Christian.
2. It is not God's will that a Christian marries a non-Christian.
3. God alone is the Source of a right marriage partner.
4. To be guided by God in choosing the right marriage partner, an individual must first be in right standing with God.
5. God guides His children in choosing the right marriage partner.

6. A marriage which is not founded upon God's principles is doomed to fail.

CHALLENGES

1. Are you contemplating marriage?
2. Are you convinced that the one you are currently dating is God's choice for you?
3. Are you in right standing with God, i.e., have you confessed your sins, forsaken them, and accepted Jesus Christ as your Lord and Savior?
4. If you are currently dating a non-Christian, are you prepared to acknowledge that you may be dating the wrong person?

3

Courtship

Courtship is the process of trying to win favor. In some societies, courtship is sometimes called dating. Marriage, on the other hand, is the ceremony entered into by a man and woman so as to live together as husband and wife. Marriage is also known by other terms, including wedding, wedlock, and matrimony. Some societies refer to dating more commonly than courtship. Dating is a social engagement in which a person enjoys activities with a partner of the opposite sex. These partners need not have any intention of marriage. Throughout this and subsequent chapters, I will refer to courtship rather than dating since the former specifically refers to partners who have declared the intention to be married. I refer to courtship as the period of time beginning when two people consent to the idea of being committed to each other in marriage until the formal marriage ceremony takes place.

The Bible presents relatively scanty information on the subject of courtship. However, we find specific principles throughout the Scriptures that are adequate to guide Christians in their manner of conduct during courtship. These principles are to override any cultural requirements that are contrary to them. To get some perspective on the duration of courtship, I will present three diverse incidences of courtship in the Bible involving the children of God.

Different Courtship Scenarios

1. Isaac and Rebekah

The complete story recorded in Genesis 24 was discussed in the previous chapter. In that story, it appears that there was no courtship between Isaac and Rebekah, since Abraham's servant who was sent to find a wife for Isaac made only a single trip away from Abraham's abode and he returned from that trip with Rebekah, the God-appointed wife of Isaac. There is no record to indicate that the couple had known each other prior to that day. In fact, the record indicates just the opposite:

> "Then Rebekah lifted up her eyes, and when she saw Isaac, she dismounted from her camel; for she said to the servant, 'Who is this man walking in the field to meet us?' And the servant said, 'It is my master.' So she took a veil and covered herself." (Genesis 24:64-65)

Perhaps, the wearing of a veil by the bride during wedding ceremonies originated from Rebekah's reaction upon seeing Isaac.

2. Jacob and Rachel

The story of the courtship between Jacob and Rachel is recorded in Genesis 29. This courtship covered a period of fourteen years, albeit, unintentionally. Laban, Jacob's uncle, had requested Jacob to serve him seven years in order to marry Rachel. After completing that obligation, however, Leah, Rachel's elder sister, was given to Jacob as his wife in a planned deception by Laban at the wedding banquet. In those days, it was the culture in that region to give the older of two sisters in marriage before the younger. Jacob, however, loved Rachel rather than Leah. Because of his love for Rachel, Jacob served Laban another seven agonizing years. Thus, it took a total of fourteen years for Jacob to be in courtship with Rachel.

3. Joseph and Mary

In Matthew 1:18-21 we read:

> "Now the birth of Jesus Christ was as follows: After His mother Mary was betrothed to Joseph, before they came together, she was found with child of the Holy Spirit. Then Joseph her husband, being a just man, and not wanting to make her a public example, was minded to put her away secretly. But while he thought about these things, behold, an angel of the Lord appeared to him in a dream, saying, 'Joseph, son of David, do not be afraid to take to you Mary your wife, for that which is conceived in her is of the Holy Spirit. 'And she will bring forth a Son, and you

shall call His name JESUS, for He will save His people from their sins."

Mary and Joseph were in courtship when Jesus was born. We have no record from the Bible of how long this courtship lasted before and after the birth of Christ, until the couple became married.

The one thing that is common to all three examples of courtship cited above is that there was no premarital sex. In the case of Isaac and Rebekah, there was no opportunity for them to engage in premarital sex since they had not known each other prior to the first day they met after the marriage ceremony that was conducted on Isaac's behalf by Abraham's servant. In Genesis 24:67 we read:

> "Then Isaac brought her into his mother Sarah's tent; and he took Rebekah and she became his wife, and he loved her. So Isaac was comforted after his mother's death."

Of Jacob and Rachel, we read in Genesis 29:27-30:

> "Fulfill her week, and we will give this one [Rachel] also for the service which you will serve with me still another seven years. Then Jacob did so and fulfilled her week. So he gave him his daughter Rachel as wife also... Then Jacob also went in to [i.e., had sexual intercourse with] Rachel."

Concerning Joseph and Mary, Matthew 1:25 states:

> "And [Joseph] did not know her [i.e., did not have sexual intercourse with Mary] till she had brought forth her firstborn Son. And he called His name JESUS."

Today, many young people are confronted with three important questions during courtship.

a. How long should courtship last?
b. Can I engage in sexual intercourse with my partner during courtship?
c. What should I do or not do during courtship?

I will answer each question based upon biblical instructions.

How Long Should Courtship Last?

As presented in the three examples of courtship above, courtship may last as short as no courtship at all (example of Isaac and Rebekah) to as long as fourteen years (example of Jacob and Rachel), or perhaps less or more than fourteen years (example of Joseph and Mary). In short, there is no specific duration recommended in the Bible that should be used universally. Because the Bible does not specifically mention how long courtship should last, every couple must prayerfully decide how long this period should last for them. Unfortunately, there is no easy answer to this question.

My personal advice is that the period should be long enough to be fully convinced that God is leading the couple to each other and to allow enough time for the couple to know each other fairly well, yet short enough to avoid the pressure of engaging in premarital sex. That period would vary from one couple to another depending on individual circumstances. The answers to the next two questions will help an individual determine an appropriate duration of courtship.

Can I Engage in Sexual Intercourse With My Partner During Courtship?

The simple and straightforward answer to this question is no. The three examples of courtship discussed above did not include premarital sex. Sexual intercourse by an unmarried person is called fornication, and by a married person is called adultery. The pleasure of sin is short-lived, but the consequences are eternal. The Bible warns God's children against this sin and its eternal consequences:

> "But fornication and all uncleanness or covetousness, let it not even be named among you, as is fitting for saints." (Ephesians 5:3)

> "Now the works of the flesh are evident, which are: adultery, fornication…of which I tell you beforehand, just as I also told you in time past, that those who practice such things will not inherit the kingdom of God." (Galatians 5:19-21)

> "Marriage is honorable among all, and the bed undefiled; but fornicators and adulterers God will judge." (Hebrews 13:4)

> "Do you not know that the unrighteous will not inherit the kingdom of God? Do not be deceived. Neither fornicators, nor idolaters, nor adulterers, nor homosexuals, nor sodomites, nor thieves, nor covetous, nor drunkards, nor revilers, nor extortioners will inherit the kingdom of God." (I Corinthians 6:9)

> "Flee sexual immorality [fornication]. Every sin that a man does is outside the body, but he who commits sexual

immorality [fornication] sins against his own body. Or do you not know that your body is the temple of the Holy Spirit who is in you, whom you have from God, and you are not your own? For you have been bought at a price; therefore glorify God in your body and in your spirit, which are God's." (I Corinthians 6:18-20)

"Nor let us commit sexual immorality [fornication] as some of them did, and in one day twenty-three thousand fell." (I Corinthians 10:8)

"Therefore put to death your members which are on the earth: fornication, uncleanness, passion, evil desire, and covetousness, which is idolatory. Because of these things the wrath of God is coming upon the sons of disobedience." (Colossians 3:5-6)

"For this is the will of God, your sanctification: that you should abstain from sexual immorality [fornication]." (I Thessalonians 4:3)

"But the cowardly, unbelieving, abominable, murderers, sexually immoral [fornicators], sorcerers, idolaters, and all liars shall have their part in the lake which burns with fire and brimstone, which is the second death." (Revelation 21:8)

I am convinced that these passages clearly indicate that premarital sex is not the will of God. Therefore, a child of God must not engage in sexual intercourse during courtship and must resist this sin into which many have fallen. For any reader who has already fallen into this sin, it is the will of

God that you confess and repent of (forsake) the sin, as God offers His forgiveness even now. You must not justify or trivialize the sin. Remember,

> *"If we say that we have no sin, we deceive ourselves, and the truth is not in us. If we confess our sins, He is faithful and just to forgive us our sins and to cleanse us from all unrighteousness. If we say that we have not sinned, we make Him a liar, and His word is not in us"* (I John 1:8-10)

In our society today, fornication is not viewed as a serious sin, but God still warns His children,

> *"You shall not follow a crowd to do evil…"* (Exodus 23:2)

THINGS TO DO DURING COURTSHIP

Courtship should be viewed as a period of acquaintance with one's partner; as the final opportunity for making sure that your partner is God's choice for you; and as the time of preparation for the marriage ceremony. Thus, every activity during this period must be carried out in light of these considerations.

First, I will discuss some things that ought to be done during courtship. Many marriages have failed because people largely ignored these activities which appeared trivial during courtship but became monsters after marriage.

1. Get to know your partner well

As often as the opportunity presents itself, observe your partner critically to identify his or her personality, likes, dislikes, reaction to situations, hobbies, and lifestyle preferences. Look beyond his or her physical appearance and focus on aspects of his or her spiritual and emotional characteristics. If possible, make notes of your observations. A potentially dangerous assumption people frequently make is that they can change their partner's personality after marriage. Nothing can be further from the truth! In fact, it is more likely that the partner would exhibit those personality traits to their full extent after marriage since, during courtship, many people try to conceal their "bad" habits and exhibit only the good to impress their partner.

If any undesirable trait shows up in your partner during courtship, do not dismiss it as irrelevant. Evaluate it in the light of your likes and dislikes and determine whether or not you are willing to put up with it the rest of your life, rather than harbor the erroneous assumption that you will change your partner after marriage. If a person is a drunkard, or smoker, or drug addict, or sexual pervert, or disorganized, lazy, filthy, or whatever, discuss these habits with your partner and see if a sincere effort is made to change of if you're willing to accept or cope with them. Compatibility should be the watchword during courtship. The more compatible partners are, the more likely it will be for them to live peacefully with each other and have a successful marriage. Remember,

"Can two walk together unless they are agreed?" (Amos 3:3)

A story is told of a wife who pressed out the toothpaste from the midportion of the tube whereas the husband preferred to push the paste from the lowermost portion. The husband got offended whenever his wife used the paste. This became a source of constant anger and conflict for the couple. Another couple disagreed over the lights in their bedroom. One partner could not sleep with lights on whereas the other could not sleep with lights off. This also became a source of constant conflict, sorrow, pain, and frustration. Observe your partner objectively without letting him or her know you are doing so. Commend the good qualities you admire in your partner, and if you have concerns, discuss them between you. Remember that your best efforts at getting to know your partner will not uncover every detail about him or her during courtship. This is why you must depend on God to lead you in choosing the right partner. If He leads you, He will give you the grace to cope and deal with any unexpected habits that show up after you have been married.

2. Discuss your aspirations and expectations

The need to discuss your aspirations and expectations with your partner during courtship cannot be overemphasized. This is an important area that is often neglected during courtship and has led to the demise of many marriages. In this discussion, honesty must be allowed to prevail. It is better to be honest about aspirations and expectations even if it may potentially result in the break-up of a relationship than to conceal facts which will ultimately ruin a marriage. Dishonesty is a very shaky foundation upon which to build a strong and lasting marriage relationship. Both physical and spiritual aspirations and expectations should be discussed.

Two important physical aspirations and expectations that are particularly worth mentioning are children and finances. You must find out what your partner thinks of children, and also share your thoughts in this matter. Some people consider children a blessing, others consider them a nuisance or a curse. Do you or your partner want children in your marriage? If yes, how many and how should they be spaced out? If one partner wants a child or children and the other does not, this must be resolved prior to exchanging the marriage vows. Someone must willingly compromise if the marriage is to work or else both partners will be unfulfilled and unhappy throughout the marriage. If both decide they want children, any known hindrances to having children must be revealed to the other partner. For example, if a man or woman has previously been diagnosed with a medical condition that precludes pregnancy, the other partner must be informed of the situation.

Possible alternatives to meeting expectations or aspirations, if any, should be discussed. A Christian lady in Nigeria had a hysterectomy prior to meeting her partner to whom she eventually became married. The man wanted to have his house full of children and made that desire known to the woman during their courtship. However, the woman failed to disclose to the man her physical condition which clearly precluded pregnancy. Several years after the marriage, all attempts to have a child failed. Both, being Christians, prayed often about the situation and trusted God for divine intervention at His appointed time. They were completely resigned to God's will and lived happily with each other.

One day, however, the woman traveled overseas and, by sheer coincidence, while searching for something else the man came across a document containing his wife's past medical history. As expected, the man became terribly disappointed by his wife's deception. He could not bear the shock and decided to end the marriage. Had the woman disclosed her medical condition to the man during courtship, perhaps they might not have married at all, or the man would have married her and been able to live with her happily, being fully aware of her situation. If she had disclosed her condition to the man and he had chosen not to have married her, I believe

God would have given both of them partners with whom they could be happily married.

If a couple chooses to have children, they should discuss how many and how the children should be spaced out. It must be remembered, however, that the best efforts at spacing out children may fail occasionally as no method of contraception is a hundred percent foolproof. Similarly, the number of children desired in a family may not necessarily be the number they may end up with. I believe that,

> "We can make our plans, but the final outcome is in God's hands" (Proverbs 16:1, The Living Bible),

and that,

> "There are many plans in a man's heart, nevertheless the Lord's counsel—that will stand." (Proverbs 19:21)

For Christian couples, the number of children they end up with, regardless of their desire, must be accepted as the Lord's will for them.

Concerning finances, there should be honest discussions about every possible aspect of finances, since more marriages have been destroyed because of disagreements over finances than any other reason. I call money the "Marriage Monster." Any believer who can put this monster where it belongs has overcome one of the greatest obstacles to a happy marriage. This has not been a conflict between my wife and me, however, as God taught us early in our marriage to put money where it belongs. Praise be to His holy name!

Learn from your partner his or her views on holding a joint account; who will be responsible for paying the bills; the importance of a budget; whether funds should be set aside for children's future education (if applicable); whether a savings account is necessary; whether parents, brothers, sisters and other members of the extended family deserve to be helped financially, and so on. Any concerns you have over money must be expressed to your partner and resolved to the satisfaction of both of you before marriage. It is advisable to seek pre-marital counseling from a Christian financial planner before marriage.

Aspirations and expectations will vary from one couple to another and can be dealt with on an individual basis. However, the principle of honesty must prevail at all times. These discussions on children and finances have been presented merely as a guide. Uncover other aspirations and expectations that are unique to you as a couple, stimulate honest discussions about them, and search for help in resolving potential conflicts before marriage.

Concerning spiritual aspirations and expectations, both partners should discuss how they would like to serve the Lord and be convinced that the partner will not constitute a serious obstacle to accomplishing each other's goals. Spiritual gifts must never be allowed to be quenched by marriage; instead, they should be augmented and used for the glory of God.

> *"But the manifestation of the Spirit is given to each one for the profit of all."* (I Corinthians 12:7)

> *"And He Himself gave some to be apostles, some prophets, some evangelists, and some pastors and teachers, for the equipping of the saints for the work of the ministry, for the edifying of the body of Christ, till we all come to the unity*

> *of the faith and the knowledge of the Son of God to a perfect man to the measure of the stature of the fulness of Christ."* (Ephesians 4:11-13)

It is good for each partner to seek to help the other realize his or her greatest potential and use the Spiritual gifts bestowed upon him or her to the fullest extent.

3. Seek premarital counseling

Every believer who is contemplating marriage ought to seek premarital counseling from a minister of God, particularly the pastor of his or her local church. God can guide you in confirming the choice of your partner through your pastor. The pastor can also assist you in planning for your wedding and offer exhortations that will help you establish your home on a solid foundation. He will pray for you and your partner and guide you through the necessary steps leading up to the marriage ceremony. In addition, he can assist you in dealing with any situation during courtship that may threaten your marriage in the future.

4. Watch and pray

Each time the partners meet together presents an opportunity for prayer. Every aspect of the courtship and the future home should be brought under the authority of the Lord. Prayer will also keep the unwed couple from sinful habits. Pray about anything and everything. You can never pray too much. Remember that a prayerless Christian is a powerless Christian, whereas a prayerful Christian is a powerful Christian. Whenever possible, make it a habit to start and end with prayer all meetings with your partner.

Things Not to Do During Courtship

Concerning things that should not be done during courtship, the greatest challenge is the temptation to engage in premarital sex. The dangers have been discussed earlier. In addition, the following consequences may follow premarital sexual activities. These in turn may threaten the marriage in the future.

1. **Premarital sex may rob you of mutual trust for each other**

    The mentality that "if he (or she) can 'do it' with me, what makes me think that he (or she) cannot 'do it' with someone else?" is bound to prevail. From the moment the unmarried couple engages in sexual activity, they will have robbed themselves of one of the most important attributes of a strong marital relationship—mutual trust! Each may begin to suspect the other of cheating. The agony of lack of trust may linger throughout the entire life of the marriage. Mutual trust and respect for each other will be stronger if the unwed couple avoids sexual relationships. There will be plenty of time for sex after marriage.

2. **Premarital sex may result in unplanned pregnancy**

    Premarital sex resulting in unplanned pregnancy can lead to a deep sense of guilt, despair, and a feeling of worthlessness and failure, even though the sin was confessed and forgiven. It will also form a basis for blaming each other, each believing that the other is the cause of the demise. A child outside wedlock will serve as a perpetual reminder of the sin—and what a painful "scar" that is!

    The following suggestions can help the unwed during courtship avoid premarital sex:

a. Avoid sleeping with your partner on the same bed

God's Word warns:

> "Therefore let him who thinks he stands take heed lest he fall." (I Corinthians 10:12)

Even if physical sexual activity does not occur, it is difficult, if not impossible, to lie in bed with a person of the opposite sex in seclusion and not think about sex. You would then be already guilty of sexual sin even in the absence of physical sexual activity. Jesus said,

> "...whoever looks at a woman to lust for her has already committed adultery with her in his heart." (Matthew 5:28)

b. Avoid caressing each other, including unnecessary hugs and provocative kisses

Anything that will stimulate one sexually should be avoided; otherwise, you will fall into sin before you know it.

c. Avoid sleeping with your partner in the same room by yourselves

During visits to each other, let the partner sleep in a separate room. If at all possible, let the partner be accommodated by a friend of the same sex, or rent a room for your partner at a hotel if you can afford one.

d. Avoid dressing provocatively

Dresses that are too revealing can be extremely tempting for men, especially when spending long hours together in seclusion. Men are easily aroused by what they see. Men and women can potentially arouse each other sexually if they dress in a manner that overly exposes the body. The Bible encourages believers to "do all (things) to the glory of God" (I Corinthians 10:31). Modesty and discretion should be considered important guiding principles for believers as they seek to glorify God even by the way they dress.

e. Avoid staying in secluded places by yourselves for too long

Such places make it conducive for activities that may ultimately lead to sexual intercourse.

SUMMARY

1. The duration of courtship depends on the issues that must be resolved prior to marriage.
2. Sex before marriage is a sin.
3. Courtship is the time to get to know your partner's personality, discuss aspirations and expectations, seek premarital counseling, and pray with your partner for your future home.

CHALLENGES

1. How long have you been dating or engaged to your partner?
2. What are your plans for getting married to the person you are currently dating or engaged to?
3. Are you currently living with a man or woman to whom you are not married? What do you plan to do about it?

4

The Marriage Ceremony

Once the couple has agreed to enter into a marriage relationship after an appropriate period of courtship, they should immediately initiate the plan for marriage. Marriage ceremonies vary from nation to nation, from culture to culture, and even from one Christian denomination to another. You should conduct your marriage ceremony in accordance with your cultural demands and local church requirements, to the extent that nothing ungodly is permitted. Remember that,

> "...*whether you eat or drink, or whatever you do, do all to the glory of God.*" (I Corinthians 10:31)

Christ must have the preeminence in everything that pertains to the marriage. For instance, if the cultural requirements include making sacrifices to idols, this must be bluntly refused and uncompromised by the child of God as it is directly at variance with God's Word, the ultimate determinant of every doctrine of the Christian faith.

In some cultures, the marriage ceremony is often preceded by an Engagement Ceremony, during which engagement rings are exchanged between the couple. It is your responsibility to determine what the cultural requirements are for you and your partner so that everything is done to

> "render therefore to Caesar the things that are Caesar's, and to God the things that are God's." (Matthew 22:21)

Make sure all key family members of the spouse that will be associated with the marriage are contacted and kept well-informed of the wedding plans. It is extremely important to seek parental consent in approving of the relationship. Remember the injunction,

> "Children, obey your parents in the Lord, for this is right. 'Honor your father and mother,' which is the first commandment with promise: 'that it may be well with you and you may live long on the earth.'" (Ephesians 6:1-3; cf Exodus 20:12; Deuteronomy 5:16)

What To Do When Parents Say "No"

In the event that either one or both of your parents vehemently oppose your relationship with your partner, it would be an act of dishonor to ignore them and proceed with the wedding. Certain facts must be borne in mind as to your course of action should either one or both parents of either partner say "no." Is the parent who is opposing the wedding a believer? If yes, it is all the more important that you ask God to confirm to you His approval of the relationship. If God indeed endorses the relationship, He will speak to the objecting parents. If an opposing parent is not a believer, you need to consider (evaluate and weigh thoughtfully) the basis for disapproval and consult with God, requesting that He speak to the parent to change his or her mind. A parent's disapproval may either represent God's means of informing you that He does not approve of a relationship that is bound to be disastrous, or a means by the devil to oppose a relationship that is potentially threatening to his kingdom. Since God cannot require you to honor your parents and simultaneously permit them to oppose the relationship, you must discern the reason for the opposition and proceed as God would lead you. Remember,

> "The king's heart is in the hand of the Lord, like the rivers of water. He turns it wherever He wishes." (Proverbs 21:1)

Therefore, if a relationship is God's will, then He can be depended upon to convince both sets of parents. God might use the parents to encourage or discourage the relationship as a means to confirm His will. In any case, neither of you should dishonor your parents—whether they are believers or not—by ignoring them and proceeding with whatever you choose to do. No parent wants anything bad for his or her child. Thus, any opposition is almost always considered by the parent to be in the best interest of the child.

You must never adopt a combative attitude toward your parent(s). My wedding was delayed by about two years because my parents (both believers) disapproved of the relationship with the woman to whom I am now happily married. The basis for their disapproval was that my wife belongs to a tribe quite different from mine and they preferred for me to marry a woman from my tribe. My wife and I were convinced at the time that our relationship was approved by God. I humbled myself before my parents and took time to explain to them that I believed she was God's choice for me and that the tribal difference would not affect our marriage relationship in any way. They were not satisfied with my explanation. My wife and I decided to pray about the situation and specifically requested that if God truly approved of our relationship, He would convince my parents so that, on their own accord, they would call and inform me that they had changed their mind. If, on the other hand, God was using their disapproval to show us His disapproval, then my parents should insist on their position.

In the meantime, we decided not to bother my parents on the issue, but rather gave ourselves unto prayer, being willing to accept whatever God's will for us was. Thus we agreed to call off our relationship and drop our marriage plans unless and until God intervened. Approximately two years after the initial disapproval, my parents informed me that after careful consideration they had become convinced that I could marry my wife. As you can imagine, my wife and I praised God for His intervention and proceeded with appropriate arrangements for marriage. Now, after more than twelve years of marriage, it seems like our marriage is only one day old—praise God! We enjoy a happy life and are forever grateful that God gave us to each other. The wait was well worth it. Had we not waited, but gone ahead to get married against our parents' wishes, I would always assume that our marriage was not God's will, especially when problems arise. However, since we were sure that our relationship was His will for us, I did not fear the days of adversity for

> "Many are the afflictions of the righteous, but the Lord delivers him out of them all." (Psalm 34:19)

Parental consent means that their blessings are upon the marriage. Proceeding to conduct a wedding despite parental disapproval may place a curse upon a marriage since it would be an act of parental dishonor.

The Wedding Ceremony

The actual wedding ceremony need not be elaborate. It is unfortunate that certain societies place unnecessary emphasis on an elaborate ceremony. Such societies consider how expensive the bridegroom's suit or bride's gown is, the number of people who attend the wedding, how much food and drinks are available at the reception, the size and quality of the wedding cake, venue of the reception, dignitaries present, etc. It is important to realize that these things do not make for a successful marriage. I have witnessed all too often such elaborate weddings that produced marriages laden with problems only days after the ceremony, many ending in divorce.

The following persons represent the minimum required for a wedding to be conducted: the bride, bridegroom, an officiating minister and two witnesses (one representing the bride's family, the other the groom's family)—five people. However, societal pressures discourage some young couples from marriage because of the feeling that if there are not many people at the wedding, then the wedding is a failure. All the other persons who attend the wedding besides these five are mere spectators or witnesses. For believers, I strongly recommend that they conduct their wedding in the presence of a minister of God, as opposed to a judge in a court of law. This is to allow the minister to pray for God's blessings upon the marriage. As you know, judges do not generally pray for the couple. They merely carry out their duties as a matter of the law.

Once the couple are pronounced husband and wife, an entirely new relationship has begun, quite different from the relationship during courtship. It is a good idea to plan for a honeymoon after the wedding to give the newlyweds a chance to be by themselves. During this time the couple may have their first sexual relationship (if they choose to). The period should be spent to relax and recover from the stress of the preparations for the wedding, and it also represents a good time to discuss intimate plans that may have been overlooked during courtship. The major expectations and aspirations of the couple should be defined at this time if this was not done earlier. Goals should be set because,

> "Where there is no vision, the people perish..." (Proverbs 29:18, KJV)

Following the wedding, the couple will begin to know each other in great detail. It will either be a time of excitement or frustration, depending on how well the couple did their homework during courtship. As pointed out earlier, be prepared for surprises. If the relationship has been God's will all along, any surprises will be easily absorbed and of little or no consequence.

The Order of Service for wedding ceremonies is as varied as the number of denominations. Fortunately, among protestant denominations, there are more similarities than there are differences.

The Roman Catholic Order of Service is slightly different from the Protestant and will not be discussed in this book. You are advised to consult with your pastor and become familiar with the specific order of service for your church. The text for the Order of Service presented below was adapted from *The Broadman Minister's Manual* (Franklin M. Segler, Nashville, TN: Broadman Press, © 1969), and from *The Christian Wedding Planner* (Ruth Muzzy and R. Kent Hughes, Wheaton, IL: Tyndale House Publishers, © 1984, 1991). Most interdenominational Orders of Service incorporate the following elements:

- Prelude
- Solo (special music)
- Processional
- Presentation of the Bride
- Call to Worship
- Hymn (or solo or special music)
- Charge
- Prayer
- Hymn
- Declaration of Intent
- Reading of Scripture
- Homily
- Exchange of Vows
- Exchange of Rings
- Prayer
- Pronouncement of Marriage
- Christ Candle
- Prayer for the Couple

- Hymn (or solo or special music)
- Benediction
- Kiss
- Presentation
- Recessional
- Postlude

Following is a brief description of some of the elements of the Order of Service listed above.

1. Presentation of Bride

The minister asks, "Who gives this woman in marriage?"

The father of the bride responds, "I do, on behalf of her mother and me."

2. The Call To Worship

The minister says, "<u>*bridegroom's name*</u> and <u>*bride's name*</u> welcome you. It is their desire that you enter into the joy, and beauty, and reverence of the following moments. Let us worship God." Alternatively, the minister may say, "Our Lord Jesus said: From the beginning of creation, God made them male and female. For this reason, a man shall leave his father and mother and be joined to his wife, so they are no longer two but one. Let us worship God."

3. The Charge

The Charge is the minister's introductory remarks that describe the nature of Christian marriage.

The minister says, "Dearly beloved, we are assembled here in the presence of God to join this man and this woman in holy marriage; which is instituted of God, regulated by His commandments, blessed by our Lord Jesus Christ, and to be held in honor among all men. Let us therefore reverently remember that God has established and sanctified marriage for the welfare and happiness of mankind. Our Savior has declared that a man shall forsake his father and mother and cleave unto his wife. By His apostles, He has instructed those who enter into this relation to cherish a mutual esteem and love; to bear with each other's infirmities and weaknesses; to comfort each other in sickness, trouble, and sorrow; in honor and industry to provide for each other and for their household in temporal things; to pray for and encourage each other in the things which pertain to God; and to live together as heirs of the grace of life." Some ministers may add, "Therefore, no one should enter this state of life unadvisedly, lightly, or wantonly; but reverently, discreetly, advisedly, soberly, and in the fear of God, duly considering the causes for which matrimony was ordained."

4. Homily

The Homily is a brief sermon. The minister says, "The home is built upon love, which virtue is best portrayed in the thirteenth chapter of Paul's first letter to the Corinthians. 'Love suffers long and is kind; love does not envy; love does not parade itself, is not puffed up; does not behave rudely, does not seek its own, is not provoked, thinks no evil; does not rejoice in iniquity, but rejoices in the truth; bears all things, believes all things, hopes all things, endures all things. Love never fails....And now abide faith, hope, love, these three; but the greatest of these is love.' (I Corinthians 13: 4-13) Marriage is a companionship that involves mutual commitment and responsibility. You will share alike in the responsibilities and the joys of life. When companions share a sorrow, the sorrow is halved, and when they share a joy, the joy is doubled. You are exhorted to dedicate your home to your Creator. Take His Word, the Bible, for your guide. Give loyal devotion to His church, thus uniting the mutual strength of these two most important institutions, living your lives as His willing servants, and true happiness will be your temporal and eternal reward."

5. Prayer

A sample prayer used by ministers after the charge or the homily is the following: "O Lord of life and love, bestow Thy grace upon this marriage, and seal this commitment of Thy children with Thy love. As Thou has brought them together by Thy divine providence, sanctify them by Thy Spirit, that they may give themselves fully one to the other and to Thee. Give them strength and patience to live their lives in a manner that will mutually bless themselves and honor Thy holy name; through Jesus Christ our Lord. Amen."

6. The Declaration of Intent

During the Declaration of Intent, the bridegroom and bride signify intent by responding to the minister's questions with a vocal affirmation. It takes place at the time that the bride is being given away. The minister says to the bridegroom, "_(bridegroom's name)_, will you have this woman to be your wedded wife, to live together after God's ordinance in the holy estate of matrimony? Will you love her, comfort her, honor and keep her in sickness and in health; in adversity and prosperity, and forsaking all others, keep only unto her, so long as you both shall live?" The bridegroom responds, "I will."

Then the minister says to the bride, "_(bride's name)_, will you have this man to be your wedded husband, to live together after God's ordinance in the holy estate of matrimony? Will you love him, comfort him, honor and keep him in sickness and in health; in adversity and prosperity, and forsaking all others, keep only unto him, so long as you both shall live?" The bride responds, "I will."

7. The Exchange of Vows

In place of the declaration of intent, exchange of vows may be used. Here, the bridegroom says to the bride: "I _(bridegroom's name)_ take thee _(bride's name)_ to be my wedded wife, to have and to hold from this day forward, for better for worse, for richer for poorer, in sickness and in health, to love and to cherish. According to God's holy plan, I give you my love." Likewise, the bride says to the bridegroom, "I _(bride's name)_ take thee _(bridegroom's name)_ to be my wedded husband, to have and to hold from this day forward, for better for worse, for richer for poorer, in sickness and in health, to love and to cherish. According to God's holy plan, I give you my love."

8. The Exchange of Rings

The minister states the significance of the ring, saying, "The wedding ring is a symbol of marriage in at least two ways: the purity of gold symbolizes the purity of your love for each other, and the unending circle symbolizes the unending vows which you are taking, which may be broken honorably in the sight of God only by death. As a token of your vows, you will give and receive the rings." The minister says to the bridegroom, "_(bridegroom's name)_, you will give the ring and repeat after me: _(bride's name)_, with this ring I thee wed and pledge my life and love to you (or with all my worldly goods I thee endow), in the name of the Father, and of the Son, and of the Holy Spirit. Amen."

Likewise, the bride says to the bridegroom, "I <u>(bridegroom's name)</u>, with this ring I thee wed and pledge my life and love to you (or with all my worldly goods I thee endow), in the name of the Father, and of the Son, and of the Holy Spirit. Amen."

9. Prayer

Following the exchange of rings, the minister prays the sample prayer, "Bless, O Lord, these rings to be a symbol of the solemn vows by which this man and this woman have bound themselves to each other in holy matrimony; through Jesus Christ our Lord. Amen."

10. Pronouncement of Marriage

The minister says to the congregation, "Forasmuch as <u>(bridegroom's name)</u> and <u>(bride's name)</u> have consented together in holy wedlock, and have witnessed the same before God and this congregation, and in so doing have given and pledged their vows to each other, and have declared the same by the giving and receiving a ring, I pronounce them husband and wife together, in the name of the Father, and of the Son, and of the Holy Spirit. Amen. 'Therefore what God has joined together, let not man separate.'" (Matthew 19:6)

11. Christ Candle

This element of the Order of Service is optional. The Christ Candle is sometimes called the Unity Candle. In the Order of Service, the Christ Candle may be placed either following the exchange of rings or after pronouncement of marriage. The minister says to the couple, "Inasmuch as Christ is the Light of the world, and inasmuch as He reigns in your hearts and it is your desire that your lives burn as one flame for Him, bringing light and life to a dark world—will you now portray your desire."

12. Prayer for the Couple

Following the pronouncement of marriage, some ministers pray for the couple, whereas others, along with the congregation, recite the Lord's prayer.

13. Benediction

The minister recites either Numbers 6:24-26 or II Corinthians 13:14. These passages are as follows: "The Lord bless you and keep you; the Lord make His face shine upon you, and be gracious to you; the Lord lift up His countenance upon you, and give you peace" (Numbers 6:24-26) and, "The grace of the Lord Jesus Christ, and the love of God, and the communion of the Holy Spirit be with you all. Amen." (II Corinthians 13:14)

14. Presentation

The minister says, "May I present Mr. and Mrs. _(bridegroom's last name)_."

Note:

The Order of Service was included in this book to acquaint the reader with the vows commonly exchanged during a wedding ceremony and to provide an opportunity for an intending couple to preview these vows and commit themselves to living by them through God's help. Vows are serious undertakings before God. Remember,

> "It is a snare for a man to devote rashly something as holy, and afterward to reconsider his vows." (Proverbs 20:25)

SUMMARY

1. It is important to seek parental consent prior to marriage.

2. When parents do not agree with your choice of a marriage partner and you are convinced that your choice is God's will, pray that God will change their heart.
3. The minimum number of people required for a wedding is five, i.e., the bride, bridegroom, an officiating minister, and two witnesses (one each, representing the families of the bride and bridegroom).

CHALLENGES

1. Are your parents opposed to your choice of a marriage partner? If so, what are their reasons?
2. What are your plans to convince your parents that you believe the partner you have chosen is God's will for you?

5

Administrative Set-up of the Home

In order for any establishment on earth to be administered efficiently, there must be a clearly defined set-up for governing the establishment. An establishment or institution that lacks an administrative set-up is guaranteed or doomed to fail. Schools, churches, nations, aviation, hospitals, etc., are examples of establishments that have a clearly defined administrative set-up. Imagine the chaos if a medical center had no administrator, was not divided into separate units (e.g., pediatrics, psychiatry, pathology, obstetrics/gynecology, emergency medical services, pharmacy, etc.), and did not have defined job duties for physicians, nurses, medical laboratory technologists, janitors, etc.

Just as other establishments cannot succeed without a defined set-up, marriage—an institution initiated and ordained by God—cannot succeed without a clearly defined set-up. God Himself has defined the rules by which the game of marriage must be played. No one can play football, basketball or baseball by his or her own rules; the games must be played by established rules. By the same token, marriage must be run by the rules of Him who set it up—God! Many marriages have failed simply because they were run by arbitrarily defined rules that suited their players rather than those set by God, the designer of marriage. God's Word declares:

> "But I want you to know that the head of every man is Christ, the head of woman is man, and the head of Christ is God." (I Corinthians 11:3; cf. Ephesians 5:23)

This passage unravels the administrative set-up of the home. Any attempt to distort this divine administrative structure could only lead to failure. The man is the head of the woman but he is not the ultimate head of the home. The man is the physical head but not the spiritual head of the home. God is the ultimate head of the Christian home. Christ is submissive unto God. Man is expected to be submissive unto Christ, as is the woman unto man. A man who is submissive unto Christ will make a godly husband, for he will know how to be the "good shepherd" of his home. God offers guidance and wisdom to such a man through Christ.

A man ought to look unto Christ constantly for guidance in carrying out his role as the head of his home. Unfortunately, many homes have no room for Christ. Such homes are founded

Administrative Set-up of the Home

upon a weak foundation and will easily collapse when they come under the least pressure. Any home that recognizes and upholds the divine administrative structure is truly blessed. Before a woman agrees to marry a man, she needs to convincingly answer the following question: "Is this the kind of man I desire to rule over my house?" If you fail to answer in the affirmative, please, stop and think, for that signals potential danger.

The administrative structure of the home invariably dictates that specific functions be carried out by each member of the family—man, woman, and child/children (if any). Just as each player on a team serves a specific function in order for the team to play the game effectively, every member of the family must serve specific functions for a marriage to be successful. The failure of any member of a team to carry out assigned responsibilities effectively will result in confusion, team frustration and ultimate failure. This is also true of marriage. The duties of each member of the family will be discussed in succeeding chapters.

Therefore, the man is the head (leader) of the home, the woman is his helper (assistant to the head), and children are the products of their relationship. God and Christ are the spiritual and ultimate rulers of the home.

SUMMARY

1. The husband has been appointed by God to lead the home.
2. God is the ultimate Head of the home.

CHALLENGES

1. If married, what is the administrative set-up of your home? If your home is not set up according to God's instruction, what do you plan to do about it?

2. If not married, what are your expectations of the administrative set-up of your home? Are your expectations similar to God's? If different, what are your plans to align your expectations with God's?

6

Duties of a Man in the Home

God has placed specific responsibilities upon the man. Without the full cooperation of the woman, the man will not be able to effectively carry out those duties. There are three areas in which a man plays key roles in the home—as a leader, as a husband to his wife, and as a parent to his child/children, if any. Only the duties of a man as a leader and as a husband will be discussed in this chapter. The parental duties of a man will be discussed in Chapter eight, along with the parental duties of a woman. Some of the topics discussed in Chapters 6-9 were adapted from the *Topical*

Analysis of the Bible (Walter A. Elwell and Douglas Buckwalter [eds.], Grand Rapids, MI: Baker Book House, © 1991), and from the Condensed Cyclopedia of Topics and Texts in the *Thompson Chain-Reference Bible* (Frank Charles Thompson, Indianapolis, IN: B.B. Kirkbride Bible Co., Inc., © 1988).

DUTIES OF A MAN AS LEADER

The primary responsibility of a man in the home is to provide leadership for his family. According to Webster's dictionary, leadership means "to go ahead so as to show the way" and, "to control the affairs or actions of." God created in man the ability to rule when He made the following solemn declaration to Eve after she and Adam had sinned against God:

> "To the woman He said...Your desire shall be for your husband, and he shall rule over you." (Genesis 3:16)

Thus, man's leadership position in the home is God-appointed, not man's design. It is not surprising, therefore, that a man—a believer or an unbeliever—will resist any attempt by a woman to rule over him, as this is contrary to his very nature. Some may view the man as a chauvinist in his leadership over the woman, but the believer must view it differently—as something that God instituted. Leadership, however, must not be viewed by believers as it is by unbelievers. Christ is the perfect example of a Leader and, if men would be strong leaders of their homes, they must follow the footsteps of Christ in this area and be obedient to His teachings on the subject. Leadership must be defined within the context of service, vision, and accountability. Let us examine the qualities of good leadership.

1. Leadership in service

Most men equate leadership with authoritarianism (blind submission and absolute, unquestioned obedience to authority), autocracy (government by one person who has unlimited power), or dictatorship (absolute authority and supreme governmental powers). They believe that being a leader means being the commander-in-chief or one who must be obeyed or whose will must be carried out without question. This erroneous perception of leadership by men is the very reason women resent men's authority over them. Some couples actually exhibit a master-slave relationship instead of the loving relationship God intended for them. Jesus taught His disciples the true meaning of leadership:

> *"But Jesus called them [His disciples] to Himself and said, 'You know that the rulers of the Gentiles lord it over them [i.e., are dictators], and those who are great exercise authority over them [i.e., are authoritarians or autocrats]. Yet it shall not be so among you; but whoever desires to become great among you, let him be your servant. And whoever desires to be first among you, let him be your slave—just as the Son of Man [i.e., Christ] did not come to be served, but to serve, and to give His life a ransom for many."* (Matthew 20:25-28)

Jesus made the above statement following the unexpected request by the mother of James and John, two of Jesus' twelve disciples, that her two sons might sit, one on Christ's right hand and the other on His left, in His kingdom (Matthew 20:20-21). She believed that those positions would give her sons unlimited power over the other disciples and over the other subjects of the kingdom. The request only aroused the anger of the other ten disciples against the two (Matthew 20:24). Jesus taught a similar principle of leadership when he washed His disciples' feet (John 13:2-11). He subsequently told them:

> "You call Me Teacher and Lord, and you say well, for so I am. If I then, your Lord and Teacher, have washed your feet, you also ought to wash one another's feet. For I have given you an example, that you should do as I have done to you. Most assuredly, I say to you, a servant is not greater than his master; nor is he who is sent greater than he who sent him. If you know these things, happy are you if you do them." (John 13:13-17)

Similarly,

> "At that time the disciples came to Jesus, saying, 'Who then is the greatest in the kingdom of heaven?' And Jesus called a little child to Him, set him in the midst of them, and said, …whoever humbles himself as this little child is the greatest in the kingdom of heaven." (Matthew 18:1-4)

By these illustrations, Jesus taught His disciples that the true mark of leadership lies in humility and service rather than lordship. A good husband must be humble and serve his wife and children, the people he leads, placing their needs and comfort ahead of his. This is what true leadership is. Jesus said,

> "I am the good shepherd. The good shepherd gives His life for the sheep." (John 10:11)

A man is the shepherd of his home; therefore, he ought to lay down his life for his family by serving them. Christ, who is described as the "head of the church" (Ephesians 5:23), taught that leadership means service.

2. Leadership in vision

A good leader is a person of vision or foresight.

> "Where there is no vision, the people perish..." (Proverbs 29:18, KJV)

Jesus stressed the importance of foresight for a leader when he said,

> "If the blind leads the blind, both will fall into a ditch" (Matthew 15:14)

How sad that many men have led their families into destruction because of their spiritual blindness! This is just another reason some women have attempted to assume the leadership of their homes. It is also another reason why a Christian sister must not marry an unbelieving husband. The husband is to set the goals and standard of conduct for the family—and that, by his living example! If a man lacks foresight, a woman must stay far away from marrying him, else she would be putting herself in an uncomfortable situation. The husband must direct the course of the family and bring or tend the family to a definite result. For example, the husband ought to take the initiative of leading family devotions. How could an unbelieving husband do that? Furthermore,

> "When the righteous are in authority, the people rejoice; but when a wicked man rules, the people groan."
> (Proverbs 29:2)

3. Leadership in accountability

A leadership position is one of stewardship and, therefore, one that requires accountability and responsibility.

> "Moreover it is required in stewards that one be found faithful." (I Corinthians 4:2)

As the sole custodian of the home, the man is accountable to his family and, more so, to God for his actions. The success or failure of any organization depends to a great extent on the leader; thus, the success or failure of marriage depends largely on the man. Whatever the man does or whichever direction he leads his family must be accomplished within the context of being accountable. Therefore, God will hold the man accountable for the success or failure of his marriage. Regardless of what the subjects do, the leader of an organization is usually the one credited with its success or failure.

From a spiritual point of view, a good leader must possess certain qualities. A few examples of such qualities follow. A good husband:

a. is focused or goal-oriented;
b. is a living example of the qualities he desires to see in the members of his family;
c. is able to accept criticism and counsel;
d. guides his affairs with discretion, weighing the consequences of his actions;

e. is God-fearing;
f. is always there for the person(s) being led;
g. places the welfare of his family above his;
h. is an intercessor;
i. is trustworthy; and
j. is courageous.

The above qualities were exemplified by Moses in the Old Testament while leading the children of Israel from Egypt *en route* to the promised land, and by our Lord Jesus Christ in the New Testament while leading His disciples during His ministry on earth. Every man ought to aspire to be the sole provider for his family, set goals and standards for his family under God's guidance, and be the watchman and spiritual leader of his home. A man who possesses these qualities will truly be a blessing to his family.

Duties of a Man As Husband

Every husband has specific responsibilities to his wife. Faithful discharge of those responsibilities makes a wife happy and, invariably, leads to a happy home. Failure to do so leads to the exact opposite effects. The following are some important responsibilities of husbands to their wives:

1. Husbands must love their wives

Every Christian husband ought to learn by heart the defining characteristics of love as detailed in I Corinthians 13:4-8:

> *"Love suffers long and is kind; love does not envy; love does not parade itself, is not puffed up; does not behave rudely, does not seek its own, is not provoked, thinks no*

evil; does not rejoice in iniquity, but rejoices in the truth; bears all things, believes all things, hopes all things, endures all things. Love never fails..."

If every man were to uphold these attributes of love and apply them to his home, there would not be a single marriage that would fail because of the man. Every husband needs to ask himself the following questions: Am I impatient with and unkind to my wife? Am I envious of my wife? Do I parade (show-off) myself before my wife? Am I puffed up (proud or arrogant)? Do I behave rudely to my wife? Do I always seek for things to be done my way? Am I easily upset with my wife? Do I think evil toward my wife? Do I rejoice whenever my wife makes mistakes or does something wrong? Do I fail to commend my wife whenever she does something commendable or right? Do I fail to bear all things, believe all things, hope all things and endure all things pertaining to my wife?

If you answer one or more of these questions in the affirmative, you have failed the test of love—you really do not love your wife! The reason you always complain about your wife and find many faults with her is because you do not love her. There is a common saying that "faults are fat when love is thin." While most men have committed to memory Ephesians 5:22-24, they stop short of proceeding further through verses 25-33 of the same passage. Ephesians 5:22-24 reads:

"Wives, submit to your own husbands, as to the Lord. For the husband is head of the wife, as also Christ is head of the Church; and He is the Savior of the body. Therefore, just as the church is subject to Christ, so let the wives be to their own husbands in everything."

However, Ephesians 5:25-33, a much longer passage, reads as follows:

> "Husbands, love your wives, just as Christ also loved the Church and gave Himself for it, that He might sanctify and cleanse it with the washing of water by the word, that He might present it to Himself a glorious church, not having spot or wrinkle or any such thing, but that it should be holy and without blemish. So husbands ought to love their own wives as their own bodies; he who loves his wife loves himself. For no one ever hated his own flesh, but nourishes and cherishes it, just as the Lord does the church. For we are members of His body, of His flesh and of His bones. 'For this reason a man shall leave his father and mother and be joined to his wife, and the two shall become one flesh.' This is a great mystery, but I speak concerning Christ and the church. Nevertheless let each one of you in particular so love his own wife as himself, and let the wife see that she respects her husband."

The need for husbands to love their wives is further stressed in Colossians 3:19:

> "Husbands, love your wives and do not be bitter toward them."

Let every man reexamine himself and determine whether he really loves his wife or not. If he does not, he has probably just identified one of the greatest causes of problems in his home. Let him repent and begin afresh a loving relationship with his wife. The results will be instantaneous. God has created the woman to be sensitive to love and the man to be sensitive to submissiveness. Both of these qualities are mutually dependent. A wife that is loved by her husband finds it easy to be submissive to him and vice versa.

2. Husbands must please their wives

To please someone is to give pleasure or satisfaction to that person.

> "But he who is married cares about the things of the world—how he may please his wife." (I Corinthians 7:33)

Once married, a husband is bound to place the interests of his wife above his own interests.

> "Let nothing be done through selfish ambition or conceit, but in lowliness of mind let each esteem others better than himself. Let each of you look out not only for his own interests, but also for the interests of others." (Philippians 2:2-3)

Many men are selfish, having the notion that their wives are simply objects of their satisfaction. Women have emotions just like men, and these emotions must be safeguarded by their husbands. Every husband ought to look out for the interests of his wife if he desires to have a lasting and satisfying relationship.

3. Husbands must praise their wives

Many men do not appreciate their wives. They fail to notice the daily routines their wives undertake to make life better for the entire family—cleaning the house, dressing the bed, washing clothes and dishes, cooking, bathing and dressing the children, grocery shopping, etc. A lot of men take these tasks for granted, yet they are arduous and energy/time-consuming. It is unfortunate that many wives do not get help from their husbands in carrying out these chores because of the erroneous mentality that these are women's tasks.

In the present generation, many wives work as much as, if not more than, their husbands to help support the family financially. Yet some men expect their wives to do the same tasks that they would normally do if they were full-time homemakers. After a woman has worked some eight or more hours away from the home each day and has single-handedly undertaken household chores, sometimes with no assistance whatsoever from her husband, a husband may still expect her to satisfy his sexual need at the end of the day. Should the wife complain that she is tired, the husband may get angry or threaten her with ill-treatment. This is nothing but selfishness!

Every human being deserves some praise in appreciation for things done to promote others' well-being. Husbands and children ought to praise their wives and mothers. Speaking in respect of a virtuous woman, the writer of Proverbs states:

> "Her children rise up and call her blessed; her husband also, and he praises her: 'Many daughters have done well, but you excel them all.' Charm is deceitful and beauty is vain, but the woman who fears the Lord, she shall be praised. Give her of the fruit of her hands, and let her own works praise her in the gates." (Proverbs 31:28-31)

A virtuous woman is, indeed, a blessing to any home and is to be praised!

4. Husbands must comfort their wives

A husband and wife need each other at all times but, particularly, during periods of distress. The Word of God states that

> *"Two are better than one, because they have a good reward for their labor. For if they fall, one will lift up his companion. But woe to him who is alone when he falls, for he has no one to help him up. Again, if two lie down together, they will keep warm; but how can one be warm alone? Though one may be overpowered by another, two can withstand him. And a threefold cord is not quickly broken."* (Ecclesiastes 4:9-12)

Whenever a woman is downcast, her husband must do everything possible to encourage her and be supportive so as to uplift her spirit.

5. Husbands must respect their wives

It may come as a surprise to many men that they ought to respect their wives. The word "respect" means to "treat with high or special regard." In many cultures, women are considered second-class citizens, i.e., of a lower social status than men. Therefore, they do not deserve to be treated with high or special regard. To do so would be considered a sign of weakness on the part of any husband. God's Word, however, teaches Christian husbands to show a different attitude toward their wives. Husbands and wives are supposed to show respect for each other at all times. Husbands, in particular, are enjoined to be sensitive to their wives' emotional needs, for wives are the weaker vessels.

Duties of a Man in the Home

> *"Likewise you husbands, dwell with them with understanding, giving honor to the wife, as to the weaker vessel, and as being heirs together of the grace of life, that your prayers may not be hindered."* (I Peter 3:7)

It is an act of disrespect for a husband to discuss his wife's weaknesses and glory in them before his friends. However, that is exactly what some men do, especially when they are with their friends and other women whom they consider to be "better" than their wives. This does not suggest that a man should not seek help in dealing with his wife's weaknesses, but it must be done in love, not with an intention to put her down before other people. After all, the man saw those weaknesses in her and yet chose to marry her. Many men find a lot of faults with their wives while overlooking their own faults. While we constantly strive to see that other people are perfect, we often fail to see our own imperfections. We see the mistakes of others while failing to notice ours. Jesus said,

> *"And why do you look at the speck in your brother's eye, but do not consider the plank in your own eye? Or how can you say to your brother, 'Let me remove the speck out of your eye'; and look, a plank is in your own eye? Hypocrite! First remove the plank from your own eye, and then you will see clearly to remove the speck out of your brother's eye."* (Matthew 7:3-5)

Whenever a man treats his wife with respect, he treats himself with respect also, for he and his wife are one.

5. Husbands must enjoy their wives

> *"Live joyfully with the wife whom you love all the days of your vain life which He [God] has given you under the sun, all your days of vanity; for that is your portion in life and in the labor which you perform under the sun."* (Ecclesiastes 9:9)

A man ought to enjoy being with his wife, spending time with her, and having fellowship with her. Unfortunately, many men spend more time outside than inside their home, thereby missing a great deal of opportunity to enjoy their families.

6. Husbands must be intimate with their wives

> *"Nevertheless, because of sexual immorality, let each man have his own wife, and let each woman have her own husband. Let the husband render to his wife the affection due her, and likewise also the wife to her husband. The wife does not have authority over her own body, but the husband does. And likewise the husband does not have authority over his own body, but the wife does. Do not deprive one another except with consent for a time, that you may give yourselves to fasting and prayer; and come together again so that Satan does not tempt you because of your lack of self-control"* (I Corinthians 7:2-5)

In order for a couple to fulfill two of the purposes of marriage—procreation and satisfaction of sexual desires—they must come together in sexual intimacy. Instead of enjoying intimacy together, some couples use their sexuality as an object of punishment. This is more common with women who deny their husbands sex for failure to satisfy their demands for other things, although men are not altogether exculpated. This ought not to be so, for sexual intercourse is supposed to be the highest level of physical intimacy, whereby a couple is literally locked together, flesh-to-flesh. Sex is a gift from God to people who are married. It must be received with thanksgiving from Him and used by a married couple for the satisfaction of their sexual desires.

7. Husbands must remain faithful to their wives

Once married, a couple is expected to remain with, and be faithful to, each other as long as they both live. After all, they both took an oath to live together, regardless of circumstances, till death do them part. Many couples have broken their marriage vows. While God does forgive sins—including marital unfaithfulness—the consequences may be grave and the scar permanent. Some women have left their husbands because the latter have been unfaithful and vice versa. In fact, the only legitimate ground for any person to divorce his or her spouse is marital infidelity. Jesus said,

> "Furthermore it has been said, 'Whoever divorces his wife, let him give her a certificate of divorce.' But I say to you that whoever divorces his wife for any reason except sexual immorality causes her to commit adultery; and whoever marries a woman who is divorced commits adultery." (Matthew 5:31-32)

Couples must do everything possible to preserve their marriage vows and the trust that they have for each other. Unfaithfulness—even if it occurs only once—erodes mutual trust to the extent that it may affect all areas of the marriage. In the majority of cases, men are the ones who are unfaithful to their wives, perhaps because they have more opportunities to be away from the home and for longer periods than their wives. As indicated elsewhere in this book, sexual intercourse outside marriage is considered a serious offense by God. Some Bible passages that point to this sin include the following:

"You shall not commit adultery." (Exodus 20:14)

"Drink water from your own cistern, and running water from your own well. Should your fountains be dispersed abroad, streams of water in the streets? Let them be only your own, and not for strangers with you. Let your fountain be blessed, and rejoice with the wife of your youth. As a loving deer and a graceful doe, let her breasts satisfy you at all times; and always be enraptured with her love. For why should you, my son, be enraptured by an immoral woman, and be embraced in the arms of a seductress? For the ways of man are before the eyes of the Lord, and He ponders all his paths." (Proverbs 5:15-21)

"And this is the second thing you do: You cover the altar of the Lord with tears, with weeping and crying; so He does not regard the offering anymore, nor receive it with good will from your hands. Yet you say, 'For what reason?' Because the Lord has been witness between you and the wife of your youth, with whom you have dealt treacherously; yet she is your companion and your wife by covenant. But did He not make them one, having a remnant of the Spirit? And why one? He seeks godly offspring. Therefore take heed to your spirit, and let none deal treacherously with the wife of his youth." (Malachi 2:13-15)

Sexual immorality has been, still is, and will continue to be sinful in the sight of God, no matter what our society thinks of it.

Summary

1. The leadership duties of a man include service, vision, and accountability.
2. As a husband, a man must love, please, praise, comfort, respect, enjoy, be intimate with, and remain faithful to his wife.

Challenges

1. As a man, how do you see your role as a leader and as a husband?
2. If your views of the duties of a man or husband are different from God's, what do you plan to do to reconcile the views?

6

Duties of a Woman in the Home

Needless to say that a woman's role in the home is paramount to the success of the home. No wonder the secular world calls the woman a "homemaker." Most people believe that a home is only as good as the woman makes it and, to some extent, that is true. The reason is obvious: she spends the greatest amount of time in the home, compared with her husband and other members of the family. Society is changing rapidly and it is now commonplace to find men spending more time at home than women. Nonetheless, the woman plays such vital roles in the home that she is an indispensable member of the family.

As was discussed for men, the duties of a woman in the home will be described relative to her roles as a wife to her husband and as a parent to her children. Her parental duties will be discussed in the next chapter, along with parental duties of the man. Many of the duties of a man as husband equally apply to the woman as wife. Where such similarities exist, they will be discussed only briefly in this section. The reader is encouraged to refer to the appropriate section in Chapter Seven, pertaining to men, where it was presented in-depth.

DUTIES OF A WOMAN AS WIFE

1. Wives must help their husbands

The primary role of a wife to her husband is to be his helper. Indeed, it is the very reason God created the woman.

> *"And the Lord God said, It is not good that the man should be alone; I will make him a helper comparable to him."* (Genesis 2:18)

The dictionary definition of helper is "one that assists." The woman thus serves to assist her husband in all his undertakings. Unfortunately, many women have turned out to be stumbling blocks rather than helpers to their husbands. This ought not to be so. A woman should ask herself: "Do I encourage my husband in carrying out his daily tasks of running the home, or do I oppose the things he does?" A woman's role in helping her husband is that of lending support to him, not taking over the leadership of the home—an act that most men resist naturally. Some women have challenged the leadership position of their husbands while others have gone even farther to overthrow them violently.

The leadership position of a man in the home is God-given and the woman must not protest it as long as the man operates within the boundary of God's will. Whenever a woman helps her husband, the latter will discharge his duties better. A most important but often neglected area of help for the man is praying for God's wisdom upon one's husband to lead the family aright. A woman can bring a lot of joy into her home by willingly helping her husband, and doing so as an act of service—not unto her husband, but unto God.

2. Wives must be submissive to their husbands

There is perhaps no other duty of wives to their husbands that has attracted greater attention, controversy, and opposition than that of her submissiveness to her husband. Such is the case when one's attention to the matter is only a pre-formed notion acquired from society's perception rather than divine injunction. Words used in place of submissiveness include subjection and obedience. To submit is to yield (to the leadership or authority of one's husband). To be in subjection is to be under the authority of another (one's husband). And to obey is to follow the commands or guidance of another (one's husband). Examine carefully the following Bible passages related to the subject:

> "Wives, submit to your own husbands, as to the Lord. For the husband is the head of the wife, as also Christ is head of the church; and He is the Savior of the body. Therefore, just as the church is subject to Christ, so let the wives be to their own husbands in everything." (Ephesians 5:22-24)

In this passage, women are obliged to submit or be subject to "their own husbands," not necessarily to all men on earth. Furthermore, the submissiveness is to be carried out as an act of service "to the Lord."

> *"Wives submit to your own husbands, as is fitting in the Lord."* (Colosians 3:18)

The wife's submission to her husband is not limitless; it must be done within the boundary of God's will, i.e., "as is fitting in the Lord." A big question is, to what extent should a woman be submissive to her husband? My answer is, as long as he operates within God's will as revealed in the Bible. If a man solicits the help of his wife in carrying out evil, e.g., stealing, killing, bearing false witness, worshipping other gods, injustice, etc., she must not lend such support. Ananias, one of the early believers, connived with his wife to lie about the sale of their possession and Sapphira submitted to him. This is an example of an instance when a woman must not be subject to her husband.

> *"But a certain man named Ananias, with Sapphira his wife, sold a possession. And he kept back part of the proceeds, his wife also being aware of it, and brought a certain part and laid it at the apostles' feet. But Peter said, 'Ananias, why has Satan filled your heart to lie to the Holy Spirit and keep back part of the price of the land for yourself? While it remained, was it not your own? And after it was sold, was it not in your own control? Why have you conceived this thing in your heart? You have not lied to men but to God.' Then Ananias, hearing these words, fell down and breathed his last. So great fear came upon all those who heard these things. And the young men arose and wrapped him up, carried him out, and buried*

> him. Now it was about three hours later when his wife came in, not knowing what had happened. And Peter answered her, 'Tell me whether you sold the land for so much?' She said, 'Yes, for so much.' Then Peter said to her, 'How is it that you have agreed together to test the Spirit of the Lord? Look, the feet of those who have buried your husband are at the door, and they will carry you out.' Then immediately she fell down at his feet and breathed her last. And the young men came in and found her dead, and carrying her out, buried her by her husband. So great fear came upon all the church and upon all who heard these things" (Acts 5:1-11)

A woman is not under obligation to be submissive to her husband when the husband is clearly carrying out an evil work that God would not sanction. That is what the apostle Paul meant by the phrase "as is fitting in the Lord." God must always have the preeminence in our lives, including when we discharge our roles as a husband or a wife. The husband must not be idolized to the point that a woman joins him in committing some atrocity that God detests. However, for as long as a man is discharging his duties within God's will, his wife is enjoined to be submissive to him. Failure to do so would constitute an act of disobedience, not to the man, but to God.

> "Likewise, you wives be submissive to your own husbands, that even if some do not obey the word, they, without a word, may be won by the conduct of their wives, when they observe your chaste conduct accompanied by fear. Do not let your beauty be that outward adorning of arranging the hair, of wearing gold, or of putting on fine apparel; but let it be the hidden person of the heart, with

the incorruptible ornament of a gentle and quiet spirit, which is very precious in the sight of God. For in this manner, in former times, the holy women who trusted in God also adorned themselves, being submissive to their own husbands, as Sarah obeyed Abraham, calling him Lord, whose daughters you are if you do good and are not afraid with any terror." (I Peter 3:1-6)

"The older women likewise, that they be reverent in behavior, not slanderers, not given to much wine, teachers of good things—that they admonish the young women to love their husbands, to love their children, to be discreet, chaste, homemakers, good, obedient to their own husbands, that the word of God may not be blasphemed." (Titus 2:3-5)

3. Wives must respect their husbands

A wife ought to treat her husband as one deserving of high or special regard.

"Nevertheless let each one of you in particular so love his own wife as himself, and let the wife see that she respects her husband." (Ephesians 3:33)

4. Wives must please their husbands

"An excellent wife is the crown of her husband, but she who causes shame is like rottenness in his bones." (Proverbs 12:4)

"There is a difference between a wife and a virgin. The unmarried woman cares about the things of the Lord, that she may be holy both in body and in spirit. But she who is

married cares about the things of the world—how she may please her husband." (I Corinthians 7:34)

5. Wives must love their husbands

Women are equally enjoined to love their husbands as much as men are to love their wives.

> "That they admonish the young women to love their husbands…" (Titus 2:4)

6. Wives must be intimate with their husbands

> "Nevertheless, because of sexual immorality, let each man have his own wife, and let each woman have her own husband. Let the husband render to his wife the affection due her, and likewise also the wife to her husband. The wife does not have authority over her own body, but the husband does. And likewise the husband does not have authority over his own body, but the wife does. Do not deprive one another except with consent for a time, that you may give yourselves to fasting and prayer; and come together again so that Satan does not tempt you because of your lack of self-control." (I Corinthians 7:2-5)

7. Wives must remain faithful to their husbands

The following scripture passages should be meditated upon by every woman.

> "You shall not commit adultery." (Exodus 20:14)

> "For the woman who has a husband is bound by the law to her husband as long as he lives. But if the husband dies, she is released from the law of her husband. So then if,

while her husband lives, she marries another man, she will be called an adulteress; but if her husband dies, she is free from that law, so that she is no adulteress, though she has married another man." (Romans 7:2-3)

"Now to the married I command, yet not I but the Lord: A wife is not to depart from her husband." (I Corinthians 7:10)

"A wife is bound by law as long as her husband lives; but if her husband dies, she is at liberty to be married to whom she wishes, only in the Lord." (I Corinthians 7:39)

SOME DESTRUCTIVE ATTRIBUTES OF AN UNGODLY WIFE

Marrying an ungodly wife for any reason is a sure recipe for trouble. Such a wife is bound to exhibit attributes that are destructive to her husband in particular, and her home, in general. Some of the common destructive attributes of an ungodly wife are listed below.

1. She is shameless and disgraceful

"An excellent wife is the crown of her husband, But she who causes shame is like rottenness in his bones." (Proverbs 12:4)

2. She is foolish

"The wise woman builds her house, But the foolish pulls it down with her hands." (Proverbs 14:1)

3. She is wayward

"For a harlot is a deep pit, And a seductress is a narrow well. She also lies in wait as for a victim, And increases the unfaithful among men." (Proverbs 23:27-28)

4. She is quarrelsome (contentious)

"A foolish son is the ruin of his father, And the contentions of a wife are a continual dripping." (Proverbs 19:13)

"A continual dripping on a very rainy day And a contentious woman are alike; Whoever restrains her restrains the wind, And grasps oil with his right hand." (Proverbs 27:15-16)

"It is better to dwell in a corner of a housetop, Than in a house shared with a contentious woman." (Proverbs 21:9; 25:24)

Crowning Qualities of Womanhood

Just as marrying an ungodly woman presents serious trouble for the family, marrying a godly wife brings joy to a home. Some of the crowning qualities of womanhood are listed below.

1. A devotional (prayerful) spirit

"But Hannah answered and said, "No, my lord, I am a woman of sorrowful spirit. I have drunk neither wine nor intoxicating drink, but have poured out my soul before the Lord." (I Samuel 1:15)

"Go, gather all the Jews who are present in Shushan, and fast for me; neither eat nor drink for three days, night or day. My maids and I [Esther] will fast likewise. And so I will go to the king, which is against the law; and if I perish, I perish!" (Esther 4:16)

[Elizabeth said], "Thus the Lord has dealt with me, in the days when He looked on me, to take away my reproach among people." (Luke 1:25)

> "Then Mary said, 'Behold the maidservant of the Lord! Let it be to me according to your word.' And the angel departed from her." (Luke 1:38)

> "And Mary said: 'My soul magnifies the Lord, And my spirit has rejoiced in God my Savior.'" (Luke 1:46)

> "Now there was one, Anna, a prophetess, the daughter of Phanuel, of the tribe of Asher. She was of a band seven years from her virginity; and this woman was a widow of about eighty-four years, who did not depart from the temple, but served God with fastings and prayers night and day." (Luke 2:36-38)

Jesus told Martha,

> "But one thing is needed, and Mary has chosen that good part, which will not be taken away from her." (Luke 10:42)

Other examples of a woman with a devotional spirit are presented below:

> "Now a certain woman named Lydia heard us. She was a seller of purple from the city of Thyatira, who worshipped God. The Lord opened her heart to heed the things spoken by Paul." (Acts 16:14)

> "I commend to you Phoebe our sister, who is a servant of the church in Cenchrea." (Romans 16:1)

> "Greet Tryphena and Tryphosa, who have labored in the Lord. Greet the beloved Persis, who labored much in the Lord." (Romans 16:12)

2. Modesty

"For she [Rebekah] had said to the servant, 'Who is this man walking in the field to meet us?' The servant said, 'It is my master [Isaac].' So she took a veil and covered herself." (Genesis 24:65)

"In like manner also, that the women adorn themselves in modest apparel, with propriety and moderation, not with braided hair or gold or pearls or costly clothing, but, which is proper for women professing godliness, with good works." (I Timothy 2:9-10)

"Wives, likewise, be submissive to your own husbands, that even if some do not obey the word, they, without a word, may be won by the conduct of their wives, when they observe your chaste conduct accompanied by fear." (I Peter 3:1-2)

3. Liberality

"All the women who were gifted artisans spun yarn with their hands, and brought what they had spun, of blue, purple, and scarlet, and fine linen." (Exodus 35:25)

"She extends her hand to the poor, Yes, she reaches out her hands to the needy." (Proverbs 31:20)

"And certain women who had been healed of evil spirits and infirmities—Mary called Magdalene, out of whom had come seven demons, and Joanna the wife of Chuza, Herod's steward, and Susanna, and many others who provided for Him from their substance." (Luke 8:2-3)

> "And He [Jesus] saw also a certain poor widow putting in two mites. So He said, 'Truly I say to you that this poor widow has put in more than all; for all these out of their abundance have put in offerings for God, but she out of her poverty put in all the livelihood that she had.'" (Luke 21:2-4)

> "Then Mary took a pound of very costly oil of spikenard, anointed the feet of Jesus, and wiped His feet with her hair. And the house was filled with the fragrance of the oil." (John 12:3)

> "At Joppa there was a certain disciple named Tabitha, which is translated Dorcas. This woman was full of good works and charitable deeds which she did." (Acts 9:36)

4. Wisdom and Virtue

> "A gracious woman retains honor, But ruthless men retain riches." (Proverbs 11:16)

> "An excellent wife is the crown of her husband, But she who causes shame is like rottenness in his bones." (Proverbs 12:4)

> "The wise woman builds her house, But the foolish pulls it down with her hands." (Proverbs 14:1)

Every woman ought to know the following passage, commonly thought of as describing the virtuous (ideal) woman:

> "Who can find a virtuous wife? For her worth is far above rubies. The heart of her husband safely trusts her; So he will have no lack of gain. She does him good and not evil

Duties of a Woman in the Home

All the days of her life. She seeks wool and flax, And willingly works with her hands. She is like the merchant ships, She brings her food from afar. She also rises while it is yet night, And provides food for her household, And a portion for her maidservants. She considers a field and buys it; From her profits she plants a vineyard. She girds herself with strength, and strengthens her arms. She perceives that her merchandise is good, And her lamp does not go out by night. She stretches out her hands to the distaff, And her hand holds the spindle. She extends her hand to the poor, Yes, she reaches out her hands to the needy. She is not afraid of snow for her household, For all her household is clothed with scarlet. She makes tapestry for herself; Her clothing is fine linen and purple. Her husband is known in the gates, When he sits among elders of the land. She makes linen garments and sells them, And supplies sashes for the merchants. Strength and honor are her clothing; She shall rejoice in time to come. She opens her mouth with wisdom, And on her tongue is the law of kindness. She watches over the ways of her household, And does not eat the bread of idleness. Her children rise up and call her blessed; Her husband also, and he praises her: 'Many daughters have done well, But you excel them all.' Charm is deceitful and beauty is passing, But a woman who fears the Lord, she shall be praised. Give her of the fruit of her hands, And let her own works praise her in the gates." (Proverbs 31:10-31)

Also, consider this passage:

"Through wisdom a house is built, And by understanding it is established; By knowledge the rooms are filled with all precious and pleasant riches." (Proverbs 24:3-4)

Temptresses

Presented here are examples of women who enticed men to sin.

1. Eve

The first woman on earth enticed her husband to disobey God.

> "So when the woman saw that the tree was good for food, that it was pleasant to the eyes, and a tree desirable to make one wise, she took of its fruit and ate. She also gave to her husband with her, and he ate." (Genesis 3:6)

God, of course, blamed Adam for yielding to his wife's ungodly suggestion:

> "Then to Adam He [the Lord God] said, 'Because you have heeded the voice of your wife, and have eaten from the tree of which I commanded you, saying, you shall not eat of it: cursed is the ground for your sake; in toil you shall eat of it all the days of your life.'" (Genesis 3:17)

2. Delilah

> "So Delilah said to Samson, 'Please tell me where your great strength lies, and with what you may be bound to afflict you.'" (Judges 16:6)

3. Jezebel

> "Then Jezebel his [Ahab's] wife said to him, 'You now exercise authority over Israel! Arise, eat food, and let your heart be cheerful; I will give you the vineyard of Naboth the Jezreelite." (I Kings 21:7)

"But there was no one like Ahab who sold himself to do wickedness in the sight of the Lord, because Jezebel his wife stirred him up." (I Kings 21:25)

4. Zeresh

"Then his [Haman's] wife Zeresh and all his friends said to him, 'Let a gallows be made, fifty cubits high, and in the morning suggest to the king that Mordecai be hanged on it; then go merrily with the king to the banquet.' And the thing pleased Haman; so he had the gallows made." (Esther 5:14)

5. Job's Wife

"Then his wife said to him, 'Do you still hold fast to your integrity? Curse God and die!' But he said to her, 'You speak as one of the foolish women speaks. Shall we indeed accept good from God, and shall we not accept adversity?' In all this Job did not sin with his lips." (Job 2:9-10)

6. "Strange Women"

"For the lips of an immoral woman drip honey, And her mouth is smoother than oil; But in the end she is bitter as wormwood, Sharp as a two-edged sword. Her feet go down to death, Her steps lay hold of hell." (Proverbs 5:3-5)

7. Ungodly Women

"And say, 'Thus says the Lord GOD: 'Woe to the women who sew magic charms on their sleeves and make veils for the heads of people of every height to hunt souls! Will you hunt the souls of My people, and keep yourselves alive? And will you profane Me among My people for handfuls of barley and for pieces of bread, killing people who should not die, and keeping people alive who should not live, by your lying to My people who listen to lies?" (Ezekiel 13:18-19)

8. Herodias and Salome

"And when Herodias' daughter herself came in and danced, and pleased Herod and those who sat with him, the king said to the girl, 'Ask me whatever you want, and I will give it to you." (Mark 6:22)

9. Sarah

"Now Sarai, Abram's wife, had borne him no children. And she had an Egyptian maidservant whose name was Hagar. So Sarai said to Abram, 'See now, the Lord has restrained me from bearing children. Please, go in to my maid; perhaps I shall obtain children by her.' And Abram heeded the voice of Sarai. Then Sarai, Abram's wife, took Hagar her maid, the Egyptian, and gave her to her husband Abram to be his wife, after Abram had dwelt ten years in the land of Canaan. So he went in to Hagar, and she conceived. And when she saw that she had conceived, her mistress became despised in her eyes. Then Sarai said to Abram, 'My wrong be upon you! I gave my maid into your embrace; and when she saw that she had conceived, I became despised in her eyes. The Lord judge between you and me.' So Abram said to Sarai, 'Indeed your maid is in your hand; do to her as you please.' And when Sarai dealt harshly with her, she fled from her presence." (Genesis 16:1-6)

"Therefore she said to Abraham, 'Cast out this bondwoman and her son; for the son of this bondwoman shall *not be heir with my son, namely with Isaac.' And the matter was very displeasing in Abraham's sight because of his son.*" (Genesis 21:10-11)

GODLY WOMEN MARRIED TO UNGODLY MEN

Abigail

In I Samuel 25 Abigail is presented as the perfect example of a godly woman who had an ungodly husband. Although her husband, Nabal, was wealthy he did not know God. Through the godly wisdom of Abigail, Nabal and his servants were spared from David's anger which would have led to a massive destruction of the men. She eventually became David's wife.

SUMMARY

1. The primary role of a wife to her husband is to be his helper.
2. A wife must also be submissive to, respect, please, love, be intimate with, and remain faithful to her husband.
3. The crowning qualities of womanhood include a devotional spirit, modesty, liberality, wisdom, and virtue.

CHALLENGES

1. As a woman, how do you see your role as a wife to your husband?
2. If your views of the duties of a woman or wife are different from God's, what do you plan to do to reconcile the views?

8

Parental Duties

Raising up any child is the most challenging thing parents can do in life. Raising a godly child is even more difficult and more challenging. Once a child comes into the world through you, you have accepted a major responsibility for which you are accountable unto God. The church has to rise up as a community to raise godly children. The following are special duties incumbent upon parents. (Duties of children will be discussed in the next chapter.)

1. **Parents must teach their children**

Some of the meanings ascribed to teaching in Webster's dictionary include, imparting knowledge; causing to know the consequences of; telling or showing the fundamentals or skills (of something). God specifically stresses the need for parents to teach their children.

> *"Only take heed to yourself, and diligently keep yourself, lest you forget the things your eyes have seen, and lest they depart from your heart all the days of your life. And teach them to your children and your grandchildren."* (Deuteronomy 4:9)

> *"You shall teach them diligently to your children, and shall talk of them when you sit in your house, when you walk by the way, when you lie down, and when you rise up."* (Deuteronomy 6:7)

> *"You shall teach them to your children, speaking of them when you sit in your house, when you walk by the way, when you lie down, and when you rise up."* (Deuteronomy 11:19-21)

> *"Whom will he teach knowledge? And whom will he make to understand the message? Those just weaned from milk? Those just drawn from the breasts?"* (Isaiah 28:9)

> *"Out of the mouth of babes and nursing infants You have ordained strength, Because of Your enemies, That You may silence the enemy and the avenger."* (Psalm 8:2)

The most common excuse given by parents for not teaching their children is lack of time. While a lot of immigrants in the United States of America become entangled in the busy routines of American life, some American parents (mostly mothers) actually create time by making the supreme sacrifice of quitting their jobs to raise godly children. Although such a decision may have far-reaching consequences for the finances of an otherwise dual-income household, the pay-off is incalculable and of eternal value. Schools, day-care centers, baby-sitters, Sunday school teachers, and television cannot take over the role of parents in teaching their children. If you fail to raise your child as instructed by God then you must be prepared to face the consequences of your negligence. God's Word says,

> "...a child left to himself brings shame to his mother."
> (Proverbs 29:15)

2. Parents must train their children

To train is: to cause to grow as desired; make or become prepared or skilled; point the way to another. Training ensures that things taught are put into practice. Following are some Scripture passages on this subject.

> "And he [Moses] said to them [children of Israel]: 'Set your hearts on all the words which I testify among you today, which you shall command your children to be careful to observe—all the words of this law.' " (Deuteronomy 32:46)

> "Train up a child in the way he should go, And when he is old he will not depart from it." (Proverbs 22:6)

> "The living, the living man, he shall praise You, As I do this day; The father shall make known Your truth to the children." (Isaiah 38:19)

> "And you, fathers, do not provoke your children to wrath, but bring them up in the training and admonition of the Lord." (Ephesians 6:4)

> "But you must continue the things which you have learned and been assured of, knowing from whom you have learned them, and that from childhood you have known the Holy Scriptures, which are able to make you wise for salvation through faith which is in Christ Jesus." (II Timothy 3:14-15)

3. Parents must discipline/correct their children

Discipline is training that corrects, molds, or perfects; it also means punishment. Discipline ensures that when training does not produce the desired results, corrective measures are taken by the parent(s) to redirect the child and keep him or her on the right course. The following Scripture passages form the basis for this parental role:

> "He who spares his rod hates his son, But he who loves him disciplines him promptly." (Proverbs 13:24)

> "Chasten your son while there is hope, And do not set your heart on his destruction." (Proverbs 19:18)

> "Foolishness is bound up in the heart of a child; The rod of correction will drive it far from him." (Proverbs 22:15)

> "Do not withhold correction from a child, For if you beat him with a rod, he will not die. You shall beat him with a rod, And deliver his soul from hell." (Proverbs 23:13-14)

> "The rod and rebuke give wisdom, But a child left to himself brings shame to his mother." (Proverbs 29:15)

> "Correct your son, and he will give you rest; Yes, he will give delight to your soul." (Proverbs 29:17)

> "If you endure chastening, God deals with you as with sons; for what son is there whom a father does not chasten? But if you are without chastening, of which all have become partakers, then you are illegitimate and not sons. Furthermore, we have had human fathers who corrected us, and we paid them respect. Shall we not much more readily be in subjection to the Father of spirits and live?" (Hebrews 12:7-9)

It is ungodly to withhold discipline from children. In America, parents are sometimes held accountable by the government when they discipline their children. Yet, the same government picks up these children when they commit a crime and jails them without the parents' consent. Any law that discourages parents from disciplining their children as they deem appropriate is ungodly. Society is rapidly filling up with children who have not been appropriately disciplined by their parents; this, in turn, has led to a greater number of juvenile criminals and, ultimately, greater government spending on crime prevention and control. It would be desirable for the United States government to revisit some of the child protection laws, to guard parents against being needlessly stripped of their God-given responsibility of disciplining their children.

Disciplining a child must be motivated by parental love. Any punishment inflicted upon a child must be with discretion and not out of proportion to the offense. Every parent needs God's wisdom in deciding what punishment is appropriate for an offense; it does not necessarily have to be corporal. Examples of non-corporal punishment include depriving a child of certain privileges he or she normally enjoys, making a child do chores he or she normally dislikes, and refusing to allow a child to spend a night at a friend's house.

If corporal punishment is ever administered, it must be light and a child must not be injured in the process. Just as much as it is wrong to not punish a child for committing an offense, it is equally wrong to administer the punishment out of rage or as an act of revenge. There is a high likelihood of punishing a child out of proportion with an offense if it is carried out while a parent is enraged. Some parents have beaten their children to death under the guise of discipline. This is ungodly. Love, not revenge, must be the watchword when punishing a child.

4. Parents must provide for their children

"In all the land were found no women so beautiful as the daughters of Job; and their father gave them an inheritance among their brothers." (Job 42:15)

"Houses and riches are an inheritance from fathers..." (Proverbs 19:14)

"Now for the third time I am ready to come to you. And I will not be burdensome to you; for I do not seek yours, but you. For the children ought not to lay up for the parents, but the parents for the children." (II Corinthians 12:14)

It is the duty of parents to provide food, clothing, shelter, and education for their children. If every parent who is capable of doing this actually does so, a needless burden will not be placed on the government to provide these amenities.

5. Parents must nurture their children

To nurture is to nourish, i.e., to promote physical and spiritual growth. It is also training or upbringing, and includes provision of food and nourishment.

> "And you, fathers, do not provoke your children to wrath, but bring them up in the training and admonition of the Lord." (Ephesians 6:4)

6. Parents must control their children

Speaking about the qualifications for the office of a bishop, Paul writes,

> "A bishop then must be...one who rules his own house well, having his children in submission with all reverence." (I Timothy 3:2-4)

Likewise, for deacons, Paul writes,

> "Let deacons be the husbands of one wife, ruling their children and their own houses well." (I Timothy 3:12)

7. Parents must have compassion for their children

To have compassion is to have pity or sympathetic sorrow for someone.

> "As a father pities his children, So the Lord pities those who fear Him." (Psalm 103:13)

> "Can a woman forget her nursing child, And not have compassion on the son of her womb? Surely they may forget, Yet I will not forget you." (Isaiah 49:15)

8. **Parents must love their children**

    "*That they admonish the young women to love their husbands, to love their children.*" (Titus 2:4)

9. **Parents must pray for their children**

    King David prayed for the life of his child:

    "*The Lord struck the child that Uriah's wife bore to David, and it became ill. David therefore pleaded with God for the child, and David fasted and went in and lay all night on the ground. So the elders of his house arose and went to him, to raise him up from the ground. But he would not, nor did he eat food with them.*" (II Samuel 12:15-17)

    David also prayed for his son Solomon:

    "*And give my son Solomon a loyal heart to keep Your commandments and Your testimonies and Your statutes, to do all these things, and to build the temple for which I have made provision.*" (I Chronicles 29:19)

    Job prayed for his children regularly:

    "*So it was, when the days of feasting had run their course, that Job would send and sanctify them, and he would rise early in the morning and offer burnt offerings according to the number of them all. For Job said, 'It may be that my sons have sinned and cursed God in their hearts.' Thus Job did regularly.*" (Job 1:5)

    The writer of Lamentations states:

> "Arise, cry out in the night, At the beginning of the watches; Pour out your heart like water before the face of the Lord. Lift your hands toward Him For the life of your young children, Who faint from hunger at the head of every street." (Lamentations 2:19)

The father of a demoniac boy and the mother of a Syro-Phoenician girl besought Christ concerning their children, saying,

> "Lord, have mercy on my son, for he is an epileptic and suffers severely; for he often falls into the fire and often into the water." (Matthew 17:15)

> "The woman was a Greek, a Syro-Phoenician by birth, and she kept asking Him to cast the demon out of her daughter." (Mark 7:26)

10. Parents are to respect their children

It may seem absurd in our society to request that parents respect their children! However, the Bible teaches just that.

> "And you, fathers, do not provoke your children to wrath, but bring them up in the training and admonition of the Lord." (Ephesians 6:4)

> "Fathers, do not provoke your children, lest they become discouraged." (Colosians 3:21)

11. Parents must exhibit solicitude for their children

Jacob sent Joseph to find out how his brothers were doing in the field.

> "Then he said to him, 'Please go and see if it is well with your brothers and well with the flocks, and bring back word to me.' So he sent him out of the Valley of Hebron, and he went to Shechem." (Genesis 37:14)

Samuel said to Saul just before he was anointed king,

> "When you have departed from me today, you will find two men by Rachel's tomb in the territory of Benjamin at Zelzah; and they will say to you, 'The donkeys which you went to look for have been found. And now your father has ceased caring about you saying, 'What shall I do about my son?'" (I Samuel 10:2)

Of Absalom's safety when he was at war with his father, King David said,

> "'Is the young man Absalom safe?' Ahimaaz answered, 'When Joab sent the king's servant and me your servant, I saw a great tumult, but I did not know what it was about.'" (II Samuel 18:29)

Mordecai, while in captivity in Babylon, inquired often of Esther, his little cousin whom he had brought up and was now queen in the king's palace:

> "And every day Mordecai paced in front of the court of the women's quarters, to learn of Esther's welfare and what was happening to her." (Esther 2:11)

If a parent is not actively seeking the welfare of his or her child/children, that parent is neglecting some important God-given responsibility.

Parental Influence and Examples

1. Evil influence of parents
   a. Ahab on Ahaziah in Israel
   "Ahaziah the son of Ahab became king over Israel in Samaria in the seventeenth year of Jehoshaphat king of Judah, and reigned two years over Israel. He did evil in the sight of the Lord, and walked in the way of his father and in the way of his mother and in the way of Jeroboam the son of Nebat, who had made Israel sin; for he served Baal and worshipped him, and provoked the Lord God of Israel to anger, according to all that his father had done." (I Kings 22:51-53)

   b. Jehoram on Ahaziah in Judah
   "Ahaziah was forty-two years old when he became king, and he reigned one year in Jerusalem. His mother's name was Athaliah the granddaughter of Omri. He also walked in the ways of the house of Ahab, for his mother advised him to do wickedly." (II Chronicles 22:2,3)

   c. Children of Judah/Israel
   "And the Lord said, 'Because they have forsaken My law which I set before them, and have not obeyed My voice, nor walked according to it, but they have walked according to the dictates of their own hearts and after the Baals, which their fathers taught them,' therefore thus says the Lord of hosts, the God of Israel: 'Behold, I will feed them, this people, with wormwood, and give them water of gall to drink.'" (Jeremiah 9:13-15)

   "Thus says the Lord: 'For three transgressions of Israel, and for four, I will not turn away its punishment,

Because they sell the righteous for silver, And the poor for a pair of sandals. They pant after the dust of the earth which is on the head of the poor, And pervert the way of the humble. A man and his father go into the same girl, To defile My holy name. They lie down by every altar on clothes taken in pledge, And drink wine of the condemned in the house of their god. Yet it was I who destroyed the Amorite before them, Whose height was like the height of the cedars, And he was as strong as the oaks; Yet I destroyed his fruit above And his roots beneath. Also it was I who brought you up from the land of Egypt, And led you forty years through the wilderness, To possess the land of the Amorite. I raised up some of your sons as prophets, And some of your young men as Nazirites. Is it not so, O you children of Israel?' says the Lord. 'But you gave the Nazirites wine to drink, And commanded the prophets saying, Do not prophesy!' " (Amos 2:6-12)

"So I also raised My hand in an oath to them in the wilderness, that I would not bring them into the land which I had given them, 'flowing with milk and honey,' the glory of all lands, because they despised My judgments and did not walk in My statutes, but profaned My Sabbaths; for their heart went after their idols. Nevertheless My eye spared them from destruction. I did not make an end of them in the wilderness. But I said to their children in the wilderness, 'Do not walk in the statutes of your fathers, nor observe their judgments, nor defile yourselves with their idols. 'I am the Lord your God: Walk in my statutes, keep My judgments, and do them.' " (Ezekiel 20:15-19)

d. Herodias, on her daughter:
> "So she [Herodias' daughter], having been prompted by her mother, said, 'Give me John the Baptist's head here on a platter.'" (Matthew 14:8)

2. Good parental example

> "And it came to pass, when Solomon had finished building the house of the Lord and the king's house, and all Solomon's desire which he wanted to do, that the Lord appeared to Solomon the second time, as He had appeared to him at Gibeon. And the Lord said to him: 'I have heard your prayer and your supplication that you have made before Me; I have consecrated this house which you have built to put My name there forever, and My eyes and My heart will be there perpetually. Now if you walk before Me as your father David walked, in integrity of heart and in uprightness, to do according to all that I have commanded you, and if you keep My statutes and My judgments, then I will establish the throne of your kingdom over Israel forever, as I promised David your father, saying, 'You shall not fail to have a man on the throne of Israel.'" (I Kings 9:1-5)

> "In the twelfth year of Ahaz king of Judah, Hoshea the son of Elah became king of Israel in Samaria, and he reigned nine years. And he did evil in the sight of the Lord, but not as the kings of Israel who were before him. Shalmaneser king of Assyria came up against him; and Hoshea became his vassal, and paid him tribute money. And the king of Assyria uncovered a conspiracy by Hoshea; for he had sent messengers to So, king of Egypt, and brought no tribute to the king of Assyria, as he had

done year by year. Therefore the king of Assyria shut him up, and bound him in prison. Now the king of Assyria went throughout all the land, and went up to Samaria and beseiged it for three years." (II Kings 17:1-5)

"So Jehoshaphat was king over Judah. He was thirty-five years in Jerusalem. His mother's name was Azubah the daughter of Shilhi. And he walked in the way of his father Asa, and did not turn aside from it, doing what was right in the sight of the Lord." (II Chronicles 20:31-32)

"And he [Uzziah] did what was right in the sight of the Lord, according to all that his father Amaziah had done." (II Chronicles 26:4)

"And he [Jotham] did what was right in the sight of the Lord, according to all that his father Uzziah had done (although he did not enter the temple of the Lord). But still the people acted corruptly." (II Chronicles 27:2)

"When I call to remembrance the genuine faith that is in you [Timothy], which dwelt first in your grandmother Lois and your mother Eunice, and I am persuaded is in you also" (II Timothy 1:5)

PARENTAL WEAKNESSES AND SINS: INDULGENCE OF CHILDREN

1. Eli

"Now the sons of Eli were corrupt; they did not know the Lord. And the priest's custom with the people was that when any man offered a sacrifice, the priest's servant would come with a three-pronged fleshhook in his hand *while the meat was boiling. Then he would thrust it into the pan, or kettle, or caldron, or pot; and the priest would take for himself all that the fleshhook brought up. So they did in Shiloh to all the Israelites who came there. Also, before they burned the fat, the priest's servant would come and say to the man who sacrificed, 'Give meat for roasting to the priest, for he will not take boiled meat from you, but raw.' And if the man said to him, 'They should really burn the fat first; then you may take as much as your heart desires,' he would then answer him, 'No, but you must give it now; and if not, I will take it by force.' Therefore the sin of the young men was very great before the Lord, for men abhorred the offering of the Lord."* (I Samuel 2:12-17)

"Now Eli was very old; and he heard everything his sons did to all Israel, and how they lay with the women who assembled at the door of the tabernacle of meeting. So he said to them, 'Why do you do such things? For I hear of your evil dealings from all the people. No, my sons! For it is not a good report that I hear. You make the Lord's people transgress. If one man sins against another, God will judge him. But if a man sins against the Lord, who will intercede for him?' Nevertheless they did not heed the voice of their father, because the Lord desired to kill them. And the child Samuel grew in stature, and in favor both with the Lord and men. Then a man of God came to Eli and said to him, 'Thus says the Lord: "Did I not clearly reveal Myself to the house of your father when they were in Egypt in Pharaoh's house? Did I not choose him out of all the tribes of Israel to be My priest, to offer upon My altar, to burn incense, and to wear an ephod before Me? And did I not give to the

house of your father all the offerings of the children of Israel made by fire? Why do you kick at My sacrifice and My offering which I have commanded in My dwelling place, and honor your sons more than Me, to make yourselves fat with the best of all the offerings of Israel My people?" Therefore the Lord God of Israel says: "I said indeed that your house and the house of your father would walk before Me forever." But now the Lord says: "Far be it from Me; for those who honor Me I will honor, and those who despise Me shall be lightly esteemed. Behold, the days are coming that I will cut off your arm and the arm of your father's house, so that there will not be an old man in your house. And you will see an enemy in My dwelling place, despite all the good which God does for Israel. And there shall not be an old man in your house forever. But any of your men whom I do not cut off from My altar shall consume your eyes and grieve your heart. And all the descendants of your house shall die in the flower of their age. Now this shall be a sign to you that will come upon your two sons, on Hophni and Phinehas: in one day they shall die, both of them. Then I will raise up for Myself a faithful priest who shall do according to what is in My heart and in My mind. I will build him a sure house, and he shall walk before My anointed forever. And it shall come to pass that everyone who is left in your house will come and bow down to him for a piece of silver and a morsel of bread, and say, 'Please, put me in one of the priestly positions, that I may eat a piece of bread.' " ' " (I Samuel 2: 22-36)

"Then the Lord said to Samuel: 'Behold, I will do something in Israel at which both ears of everyone who hears it will tingle. In that day I will perform against Eli all that

I have spoken concerning his house, from beginning to end. For I have told him that I will judge his house forever for the iniquity which he knows, because his sons made themselves vile, and he did not restrain them. And therefore I have sworn to the house of Eli that the iniquity of Eli's house shall not be atoned for by sacrifice or offering forever." (I Samuel 3:11-14)

"And when the people had come into the camp, the elders of Israel said, 'Why has the Lord defeated us today before the Philistines? Let us bring the ark of the covenant of the Lord from Shiloh to us, that when it comes among us it may save us from the hand of our enemies. So the people went to Shiloh, that they might bring from there the ark of the covenant of the Lord of hosts, who dwells between the cherubim. And the two sons of Eli, Hophni and Phinehas, were there with the ark of the covenant of God." (I Samuel 4:3-4)

"So the Philistines fought, and Israel was defeated, and every man fled to his tent. There was a very great slaughter, and there fell of Israel thirty thousand foot soldiers. Also the ark of God was captured; and the two sons of Eli, Hophni and Phinehas, died. Then a man of Benjamin ran from the battle line the same day, and came to Shiloh with his clothes torn and dirt on his head. Now when he came there was Eli, sitting on a seat by the wayside watching, for his heart trembled for the ark of God. And when the man came into the city and told it, all the city cried out. When Eli heard the noise of the outcry, he said, 'What does the sound of this tumult mean?' And the man came quickly and told Eli." (I Samuel 4:10-14)

2. **Samuel**

   "Now it came to pass when Samuel was old that he made his sons judges over Israel. The name of his firstborn was Joel, and the name of his second, Abijah; they were judges in Beer-Sheba. But his sons did not walk in his ways; they turned aside after dishonest gain, took bribes, and perverted justice." (I Samuel 8:1-3)

3. **David**

   "Then Adonijah the son of Haggith exalted himself, saying, 'I will be king'; and he prepared for himself chariots and horsemen, and fifty men to run before him. And his father [David] had not rebuked him at any time by saying, 'Why have you done so?' He was also very good-looking. His mother had borne him after Absalom." (I Kings 1:6)

SUMMARY

1. Parents must teach, train, discipline, correct, nurture, control, love, respect, provide for, pray for, and have solicitude and compassion for their children.
2. Parents have a direct influence on their children. Their influence may lead children toward either good or evil.
3. Indulgence of a child is indicative of parental weakness.

CHALLENGE

1. What role are you playing as a parent?
2. How are you influencing the life of your child or children?
3. What legacy are you leaving for your child or children?

9

Facts about Children

Children are so important in the sight of God, I have devoted an entire chapter to learning about them.

CHILDREN ARE GIFTS FROM GOD

"And he [Esau] lifted his eyes and saw the women and children, and said, 'Who are these with you?' So he [Jacob] said, 'The children whom God has graciously given your servant.'" (Genesis 33:5)

"And Joseph said to his father, 'They are my sons, whom God has given me in this place.' And he said, 'Please bring them to me, and I will bless them.'" (Genesis 48:9)

"Then I took your father Abraham from the other side of the River, led him throughout all the land of Canaan, and multiplied his descendants and gave him Isaac." (Joshua 24:3)

"He grants the barren woman a home, Like a joyful mother of children. Praise the Lord!" (Psalm 113:9)

"Behold, children are a heritage from the Lord, The fruit of the womb is a reward." (Psalm 127:3)

"Here am I and the children whom the Lord has given me! We are for signs and wonders in Israel From the Lord of hosts, Who dwells in Mount Zion." (Isaiah 8:18)

Children Are Esteemed Highly

"Like arrows in the hand of a warrior, So are the children of one's youth. Happy is the man who has his quiver full of them; They shall not be ashamed, But shall speak with their enemies in the gate." (Psalm 127:4-5)

"Your wife shall be like a fruitful vine In the very heart of your house, Your children like olive plants All around your table." (Psalm 128:3)

"Children's children are the crown of old men, And the glory of children is their father." (Proverbs 17:6)

"But Jesus said, 'Let the little children come to Me, and do not forbid them; for of such is the kingdom of heaven.'" (Matthew 19:14)

Exhortations to Children

"Come, you children, listen to me; I will teach you the fear of the Lord." (Psalm 34:11)

"Both young men and maidens; Old men and children. Let them praise the name of the Lord, For His name alone is exalted; His glory is above the earth and heaven." (Psalm 148:12-13)

"Honor your father and your mother, that your days may be long upon the land which the Lord your God is giving you." (Exodus 20:12)

"The proverbs of Solomon: A wise son makes a glad father, But a foolish son is the grief of his mother." (Proverbs 10:1)

"Even a child is known by his deeds, Whether what he does is pure and right." (Proverbs 20:11)

"Listen to your father who begot you, And do not despise your mother when she is old." (Proverbs 23:22)

"Remember now your Creator in the days of your youth, Before the difficult days come, And the years draw near when you say, 'I have no pleasure in them." (Ecclesiastes 12:1)

"But I said to their children in the wilderness, 'Do not walk in the statutes of your fathers, nor observe their judgments, nor defile yourselves with their idols.' " (Ezekiel 20:18)

"For Moses said, 'Honor your father and your mother'; and, 'He who curses father or mother, let him be put to death.'" (Mark 7:10)

"Children, obey your parents in the Lord, for this is right. 'Honor your father and mother,' which is the first commandment with promise: 'that it may be well with you and you may live long on the earth.'" (Ephesians 6:1-3)

"Children, obey your parents in all things, for this is well pleasing to the Lord." (Colossians 3:20)

"But if any widow has children or grandchildren, let them first learn to show piety at home and to repay their parents; for this is good and acceptable before God." (I Timothy 5:4)

Special Promises to Children

There are special promises for godly children in God's Word.

1. **Reverent children**

    "Honor your father and your mother, as the Lord your God has commanded you, that your days may be long, and that it may be well with you in the land which the Lord your God is giving you." (Deuteronomy 5:16)

2. **Forsaken children:**

    "When my father and my mother forsake me, Then the Lord will take care of me." (Psalm 27:10)

3. **Early seekers**

    "I love those who love me, And those who seek me diligently will find me." (Proverbs 8:17)

4. **Obedient children**

    "Now therefore, listen to me, my children, For blessed are those who keep my ways." (Proverbs 8:32)

5. **Lambs of the flock**

    "He will feed His flock like a shepherd; He will gather the lambs with His arm, And carry them in His bosom, And gently lead those who are with young." (Isaiah 40:11)

6. **Little children**

    "But when Jesus saw it, He was greatly displeased and said to them, 'Let the little children come to Me, and do not forbid them; for of such is the kingdom of God.'" (Mark 10:14)

7. **Children of believers**

    "For the promise is to you and to your children, and to all who are afar off, as many as the Lord our God will call." (Acts 2:39)

8. **The commandment with Promise**

    "'Honor your father and mother,'" which is the first commandment with promise: 'that it may be well with you and you may live long on the earth.'" (Ephesians 6:2-3)

UNGRATEFUL CHILDREN

"And he who strikes his father or his mother shall surely be put to death." (Exodus 21:15)

"For everyone who curses his father or his mother shall surely be put to death. He has cursed his father or his mother. His blood shall be upon him." (Leviticus 20:9)

"If a man has a stubborn and rebellious son who will not obey the voice of his father or the voice of his mother, and who, when they have chastened him, will not heed them, then his father and his mother shall take hold of him and bring him out to the elders of his city, to the gate of his city. And they shall say to the elders of his city, 'This son of ours is stubborn and rebellious; he will not obey our voice; he is a glutton and a drunkard.' Then all the men of his city shall stone him to death with stones; so you shall put away the evil from among you, and all Israel shall hear and fear." (Deuteronomy 21:18-21)

"Whoever robs his father or his mother, And says, 'It is no transgression,' The same is companion to a destroyer." (Proverbs 28:24)

"The eye that mocks his father, And scorns obedience to his mother, The ravens of the valley will pick it out, And the young eagles will eat it." (Proverbs 30:17)

"For a son dishonors father, Daughter rises against her mother, Daughter-in-law against her mother-in-law; A man's enemies are the men of his own household." (Micah 7:6)

"But you say, 'If a man says to his father or mother, "Whatever profit you might have received from me is Corban"—' (that is a gift to God), then you no longer let him do anything for his father or mother, making the word of God of no effect through your tradition which you have handed down. And many such things you do." (Mark 7:11-13)

Facts about Children

EXAMPLES OF HELPFUL CHILDREN

1. **The child Samuel assists Eli**

   "But Samuel ministered before the Lord, even as a child, wearing a linen ephod." (I Samuel 2:18)

2. **A boy who waited upon David and Jonathan**

   "Then he said to his lad, 'Now run, find the arrows which I shoot.' As the lad ran, he shot an arrow beyond him." (I Samuel 20:36)

3. **A little maid who aided Naaman in securing his health**

   "And the Syrians had gone out on raids, and had brought back captive a young girl from the land of Israel. She waited on Naaman's wife. Then she said to her mistress, 'If only my master were with the prophet who is in Samaria! For he would heal him of his leprosy.'" (2 Kings 5:2-3)

4. **A child king**

   "Joash [Jehoash] was seven years old when he became king, and he reigned forty years in Jerusalem. His mother's name was Zibiah of Beersheba." (2 Chronicles 24:1)

5. **The boy, Christ, about his father's business**

   "And He said to them, 'Why did you seek Me? Did you not know that I must be about My Father's business?'" (Luke 2:49)

6. **The lad who gave his lunch to help feed the multitude**

   "There is a lad here who has five barley loaves and two small fish, but what are they among so many?" (John 6:9)

VICES OF CHILDREN

1. Against Elisha

"Then he [Elisha] went up from there to Bethel; and as he was going up the road, some youths came from the city and mocked him, and said to him, 'Go up, you baldhead! Go up, you baldhead!'" (2 Kings 2:23)

2. Against Job

"Even young children despise me; I arise, and they speak against me." (Job 19:18)

"At my right hand the rabble arises; They push away my feet, And they raise against me their ways of destruction." (Job 30:12)

EXAMPLES OF GOOD CHILDREN OF GOOD PARENTAGE

1. Isaac

"But Isaac spoke to Abraham his father and said, 'Here I am, my son.' Then he said, 'Look, the fire and the wood, but where is the lamb for a burnt offering?'" (Genesis 22:7)

2. Jephthah's daughter

"So she said to him, 'My father, if you have given your word to the Lord, do to me according to what has gone out of your mouth, because the Lord has avenged you of your enemies, the people of Ammon.'" (Judges 11:36)

3. Samuel

"And the child Samuel grew in stature, and in favor both with the Lord and men." (I Samuel 2:26)

4. John the Baptist

"*So the child grew and became strong in spirit, and was in the deserts till the day of his manifestation to Israel.*" (Luke 1:80)

5. The boy Jesus

"*And He said to them, 'Why did you seek Me? Did you not know that I must be about My Father's business?'*" (Luke 2:49)

6. Timothy

"*When I call to remembrance the genuine faith that is in you, which dwelt first in your grandmother Lois and your mother Eunice, and I am persuaded is in you also.*" (II Timothy 1:5)

Examples of Good Children of Wicked Men

Although the following children had wicked parents, they followed the examples of their godly ancestors rather than their wicked parents.

1. Jehoash

"*Jehoash did what was right in the sight of the Lord all the days in which Jehoiada the priest instructed him.*" (II Kings 12:2)

2. Hezekiah

"*And he did what was right in the sight of the Lord, according to all that his father David had done.*" (II Kings 18:3)

3. Josiah

> "Josiah was eight years old when he became king, and he reigned thirty-one years in Jerusalem. His mother's name was Jedidah the daughter of Adaidah of Bozkath. And he did what was right in the sight of the Lord, and walked in all the ways of his father David; he did not turn aside to the right hand or to the left." (II Kings 22:1-2)

> "Josiah was eight years old when he became king, and he reigned thirty-one years in Jerusalem. And he did what was right in the sight of the Lord, and walked in the ways of his father David; he did not turn aside to the right hand or to the left. For in the eighth year of his reign, while he was still young, he began to seek the God of his father David; and in the twelfth year be began to purge Judah and Jerusalem of the high places, the wooden images, the carved images, and the molded images." (II Chronicles 34:1-3)

DIFFERENT WAYS CHILDREN CAN DISHONOR THEIR PARENTS

1. By stubbornness and sensuality

> "And they shall say to the elders of his city, 'This son of ours is stubborn and rebellious; he will not obey our voice; he is a glutton and a drunkard.'" (Deuteronomy 21:20)

2. By lack of respect for parents

> "Cursed is the one who treats his father or his mother with contempt." (Deuteronomy 27:16)

3. **By despising their mother**

    "There is a generation that curses its father, And does not bless its mother." (Proverbs 30:11)

4. **By strife in the household**

    "For son dishonors father, Daughter rises against her mother, Daughter-in-law against her mother-in-law; A man's enemies are the men of his own household." (Micah 7:6)

5. **By failure in providing for parents**

    "But you say, 'If a man says to his father or mother, "Whatever profit you might have received from me is Corban"—' (that is, a gift to God), then you no longer let him do anything for his father or his mother, making the word of God of no effect through your tradition which you have handed down. And many such things you do." (Mark 7:11-13)

6. **By disobedience to parents**

    "For men will be lovers of themselves, lovers of money, boasters, proud, blasphemers, disobedient to parents, unthankful, unholy." (II Timothy 3:2)

SUMMARY

1. Children are gifts from God and are held in high esteem by Him.
2. God promises long life to children who are obedient to their parents.
3. A God-fearing child may come out of godly as well as ungodly parents; hence, no child can blame his or her actions entirely on poor parentage.

4. A child may dishonor his or her parents by stubbornness, sensuality, despising, disobedience to, and lack of respect, as well as causing strife in the home.

Challenge

1. How would you describe your relationship with your parent(s)?
2. Do you honor or dishonor your parent(s)?
3. If you are angry at your parents, for whatever reason, would you commit to honoring them by forgiving and reconciling with them?

10

Enemies of the Home

An enemy is one who seeks to inflict injury to another, or a hostile force or power. There are many forces that work against the home. Some of these forces are examined below.

Adultery

Marital infidelity is a major threat to any family. The Scriptures are very clear in their condemnation of this sin.

> *"You have heard that it was said to those of old, 'You shall not commit adultery.' But I say to you that whoever looks*

at a woman to lust for her has already committed adultery with her in his heart." (Matthew 5:27-28)

"And I say to you, whoever divorces his wife, except for sexual immorality, and marries another, commits adultery; and whoever marries her who is divorced commits adultery." (Matthew 19:9)

"So then if, while her husband lives, she marries another man, she will be called an adulteress; but if her husband dies, she is free from that law, so that she is no adulteress, though she has married another man." (Romans 7:3)

"Do you not know that the unrighteous will not inherit the kingdom of God? Do not be deceived. Neither fornicators, nor idolaters, nor adulterers, nor homosexuals, nor sodomites, nor thieves, nor covetous, nor drunkards, nor revilers, nor extortioners will inherit the kingdom of God. And such were some of you. But you were washed, but you were sanctified, but you were justified in the name of the Lord Jesus and by the Spirit of our God." (I Corinthians 6:9-11)

"Having eyes full of adultery and that cannot cease from sin, enticing unstable souls. They have a heart trained in covetous practices, and are accursed children." (II Peter 2:14)

"For the commandment is a lamp, And the law a light; Reproofs of instruction are the way of life, To keep you from the evil woman, From the flattering tongue of a seductress. Do not lust after her beauty in your heart, Nor let her allure you with her eyelids. For by means of a harlot a man is reduced to a crust of bread; And an adulteress will prey upon his precious life. Can a man take fire to his bosom, And his clothes not be burned? Can one walk on hot coals, And his feet not be seared? So is he who goes in to his neighbor's wife; Whoever touches her shall not be innocent." (Proverbs 6:23-29)

"Whoever commits adultery with a woman lacks understanding; He who does so destroys his own soul. Wounds and dishonor he will get, And his reproach will not be wiped away. For jealousy is a husband's fury; Therefore he will not spare in the day of vengeance. He will accept no recompense, Nor will he be appeased though you give many gifts." (Proverbs 6:32-35)

POLYGAMY

Although polygamy was an accepted social custom throughout the ancient Middle East and a common practice among God's children in ancient Israel, it is a clear deviation from God's original plan for marriage, for it is written,

"Therefore a man shall leave his father and mother and be joined to his wife, and they shall become one flesh." (Genesis 2:24)

Furthermore, God's law warned rulers against marrying many women:

"Neither shall he (a governing King) multiply wives for himself, lest his heart turn away..." (Deuteronomy 17:17)

Finally, both the Bible and human experience are replete with the tragic results of polygamy—turbulence and divided families.

The following are examples of children of God who practiced polygamy:

1. Lamech

"Then Lamech took for himself two wives: the name of one was Adah, and the name of the second was Zillah." (Genesis 4:19)

2. Abraham

"Then Sarai said to Abram, 'See now, the Lord has restrained me from bearing children. Please, go in to my maid; perhaps I shall obtain children by her.' And Abram heeded the voice of Sarai." (Genesis 16:3)

3. Esau

"When Esau was forty years old, he took as wives Judith the daughter of Beeri the Hittite, and Basemath the daughter of Elon the Hittite. And they were a grief of mind to Isaac and Rebekah." (Genesis 26:34-35)

4. Jacob

"Then Jacob did so and fulfilled her week. So he gave him his daughter Rachel as wife also." (Genesis 29:28)

5. Gideon

"Gideon had seventy sons who were his own offspring, for he had many wives." (Judges 8:30)

6. Elkanah

"Now there was a certain man of Ramathaim Zophim, of the mountains of Ephraim, and his name was Elkanah the son of Jeroham, the son of Elihu, the son of Tohu, the son of Zuph, an Ephraimite. And he had two wives: the *name of one was Hannah, and the name of the other Peninnah. Peninnah had children, but Hannah had no children."* (I Samuel 1:1-2)

7. David

"Sons were born to David in Hebron: His firstborn was Amnon by Ahinoam the Jezreelitess; his second Chileab, by Abigail the widow of Nabal the Carmelite; the third, Absalom the son of Maacah, the daughter of Talmai, king of Geshur; the fourth, Adonijah the son of Haggith; the fifth, Shephatiah the son of Abital; and the sixth, Ithream, by David's wife Eglah. These were born to David in Hebron." (II Samuel 3:2-5)

8. Solomon

"But King Solomon loved many foreign women, as well as the daughter of Pharaoh: women of the Moabites, Ammonites, Edomites, Sidonians, and Hittites—from the nations of whom the Lord had said to the children of Israel, 'You shall not intermarry with them, nor they with you. Surely they will turn away your hearts after their gods.' Solomon clung to these in love. And he had seven hundred wives, princesses, and three hundred concubines; and his wives turned away his heart." (I Kings 11:1-3)

9. Ashhur

"And Ashhur the father of Tekoa had two wives, Helah and Naarah." (1 Chronicles 4:5)

10. Rehoboam

"Then Rehoboam [Solomon's son] took for himself as wife Mahalath the daughter of Jerimoth the son of David, and

of Abihail the daughter of Eliah the son of Jesse." (II Chronicles 11:18)

11. Abijah (King of Judah):

"But Abijah grew mighty, married fourteen wives, and begot twenty-two sons and sixteen daughters." (II Chronicles 13:21)

12. Jehoiada (priest):

"And Jehoiada took two wives for him, and he had sons and daughters." (II Chronicles 24:3)

Polygamy is forbidden

"So God created man in His own image; in the image of God He created him; male and female He created them." (Genesis 1:27)

"Therefore a man shall leave his father and mother and be joined to his wife, and they shall become one flesh." (Genesis 2:24-25)

"Neither shall he multiply wives for himself, lest his heart turn away; nor shall he greatly multiply silver and gold for himself." (Deuteronomy 17:17)

"But did He not make them one, Having a remnant of the Spirit? And why one? He seeks godly offspring. Therefore take heed to your spirit, And let none deal treacherously with the wife of his youth." (Malachi 2:15)

"And He answered and said to them, 'Have you not read that He who made them at the beginning "made them

male and female," and said, *"For this reason a man shall leave his father and mother and be joined to his wife, and the two shall become one flesh"? So then, they are no longer two but one flesh. Therefore what God has joined together, let not man separate.'* " (Matthew 19:4)

"A bishop then must be blameless, the husband of one wife, temperate, sober-minded, of good behavior, hospitable, able to teach." (I Timothy 3:2)

"Let deacons be the husbands of one wife, ruling their children and their own houses well." (I Timothy 3:12)

"If a man is blameless, the husband of one wife, having faithful children not accused of dissipation or insubordination." (Titus 1:6)

DIVORCE

Divorce is defined as the legal breaking up of a marriage. A review of several issues of the *Monthly Vital Statistics Report* (Volumes 41-47, 1993-1999) show the following startling divorce statistics for the United States during the period, 1950-1998:

a. Divorces granted have increased steadily since 1950, seemingly leveled off since 1979, and reached an all-time high of 1,215,000 in 1992 (Figure 1).
b. Divorce is more frequent among couples under the age of 40 than for older married couples (Figure 2).
c. Most divorces are concentrated within the first 10 years of marriage (Figure 3).

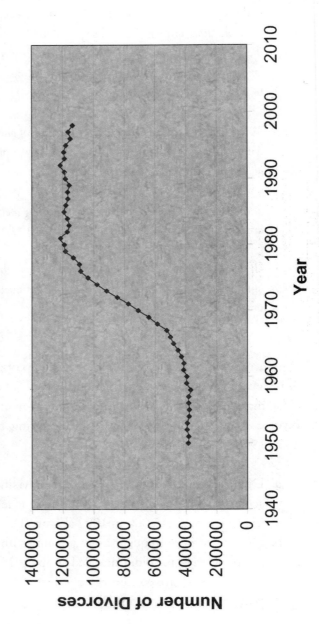

Figure 2
Age-Specific Divorce Rates for Men and Women: United States Divorce-Registration Area, 1990

(Source: *Monthly Vital Statistics Report*, Vol. 43, No. 9(S), March 22, 1995)

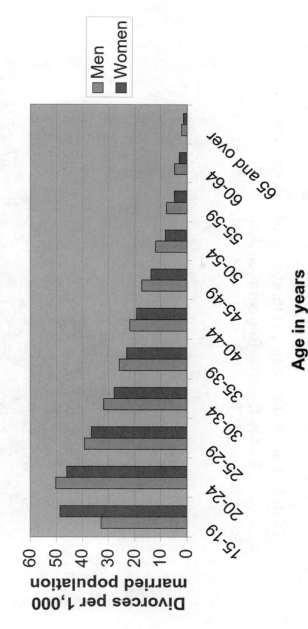

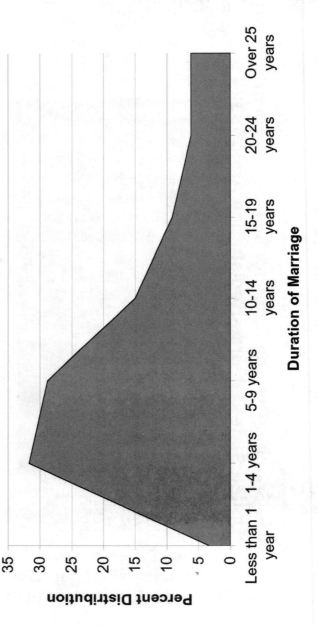

The most troubling facts about these statistics are that Christians constitute a large proportion of divorces and the number of divorces over five decades has yet to show a downward trend. Christians must rise to the challenge of reversing the divorce trend by making a commitment to remain faithful to their spouses and by keeping their vows, "till death do us part," thus serving as role models for society.

1. What is God's attitude towards divorce?

Divorce was never in God's plan when He instituted marriage. Therefore, His attitude toward divorce is one of outrage and bitterness. He hates divorce because He loves us and knows the trauma that comes with it—something He never wants us to experience. God's perfect plan for marriage is one man, one woman, for life—and it is possible to experience this plan! Consider the following Scripture passages as they relate to divorce and God's attitude towards it.

> *"When a man takes a wife and marries her, and it happens that she finds no favor in his eyes because he has found some uncleanness in her, and he writes her a certificate of divorce, puts it in her hand, and sends her out of his house, when she has departed from his house, and goes and becomes another man's wife, if the latter husband detests her and writes her a certificate of divorce, puts it in her hand, and sends her out of his house, or if the latter husband dies who took her as his wife, then her former husband who divorced her must not take her back to be his wife after she has been defiled; for that is an abomination before the Lord, and you shall not bring sin on the land which the Lord your God is giving you as an inheritance."* (Deuteronomy 24:1-4)

"*They say, 'If a man divorces his wife, And she goes from him And becomes another man's, May he return to her again?' Would not that land be greatly polluted? But you have played the harlot with many lovers; 'Yet return to Me,' says the Lord.*" (Jeremiah 3:1)

"*Surely, as a wife treacherously departs from her husband, So have you dealt treacherously with Me, O house of Israel,' says the Lord.*" (Jeremiah 3:20)

"*And this is the second thing you do: You cover the altar of the Lord with tears, With weeping and crying; So He does not regard the offering anymore, Nor receive it with goodwill from your hands. Yet you say, 'For what reason?' Because the Lord has been witness Between you and the wife of your youth, With whom you have dealt treacherously; Yet she is your companion And your wife by covenant. But did He not make them one, Having a remnant of the Spirit? And why one? He seeks godly offspring. Therefore take heed to your spirit, And let none deal treacherously with the wife of his youth. 'For the Lord God of Israel says That He hates divorce, For it covers one's garment with violence,' Says the Lord of hosts. 'Therefore take heed to your spirit, That you do not deal treacherously.' You have wearied the Lord with your words; Yet you say, 'In what way have we wearied Him?' In that you say, Everyone who does evil Is good in the sight of the Lord, And He delights in them,' Or, 'Where is the God of justice?'*" (Malachi 2:13-17)

"*Furthermore it has been said, 'Whoever divorces his wife, let him give her a certificate of divorce.' But I say to you that whoever divorces his wife for any reason except sexual immorality causes her to commit adultery; and whoever marries a woman who is divorced commits adultery."* (Matthew 5:31-32)

"The Pharisees also came to Him, testing Him, and saying to Him, 'Is it lawful for a man to divorce his wife for just any reason?' And He answered and said to them, 'Have you not read that He who made them at the beginning made them male and female,' and said, 'For this reason a man shall leave his father and mother and be joined to his wife, and the two shall become one flesh?' 'So then, they are no longer two but one flesh. Therefore what God has joined together, let not man separate.' They said to Him, 'Why then did Moses command to give a certificate of divorce, and to put her away?' He said to them, 'Moses, because of the hardness of your hearts, permitted you to divorce your wives, but from the beginning it was not so. And I say to you, whoever divorces his wife, except for sexual immorality, and marries another, commits adultery; and whoever marries her who is divorced commits adultery. His disciples said to Him, 'If such is the case of the man with his wife, it is better not to marry.' But He said to them, 'All cannot accept this saying, but only those to whom it has been given: For there are eunuchs who were born thus from their mother's womb, and there are eunuchs who were made eunuchs by men, and there are eunuchs who have made themselves eunuchs for the kingdom of heaven's sake. He who is able to accept it, let him accept it.'" (Matthew 19:3-12)

"The Pharisees came and asked Him, 'Is it lawful for a man to divorce his wife?' testing Him. And He answered and said to them, 'What did Moses command you?' They

said, 'Moses permitted a man to write a certificate of divorce, and to dismiss her.' And Jesus answered and said to them, 'Because of the hardness of your heart he wrote you this precept. But from the beginning of the creation, God made them male and female.' 'For this reason a man shall leave his father and mother and be joined to his wife, and the two shall become one flesh'; Therefore what God has joined together, let not man separate." In the house His disciples also asked Him again about the same matter. So He said to them, 'Whoever divorces his wife and marries another commits adultery against her. And if a woman divorces her husband and marries another, she commits adultery.' " (Mark 10:2-12)

"Whoever divorces his wife and marries another commits adultery; and whoever marries her who is divorced from her husband commits adultery." (Luke 16:18)

"Now to the married I command, yet not I but the Lord: A wife is not to depart from her husband. But even if she does depart, let her remain unmarried or be reconciled to her husband. And a husband is not to divorce his wife." (I Corinthians 7:10-11)

"A wife is bound by law as long as her husband lives; but if her husband dies, she is at liberty to be married to whom she wishes, only in the Lord. But she is happier if she remains as she is, according to my judgment—and I think I also have the Spirit of God." (I Corinthians 7:39-40)

"Or do you not know, brethren (for I speak to those who know the law), that the law has dominion over a man as *long as he lives? For the woman who has a husband is bound by the law to her husband as long as he lives. But if the husband dies, she is released from the law of her husband. So then if, while her husband lives, she marries another man, she will be called an adulteress; but if her husband dies, she is free from that law, so that she is no adulteress, though she has married another man."* (Romans 7:1-3)

"Remember! Do not forget how you provoked the Lord your God to wrath in the wilderness. From the day that you departed from the land of Egypt until you came to this place, you have been rebellious against the Lord." (Deuteronomy 9:7)

"Thus says the Lord: 'Stand in the ways and see, And ask for the old paths, where the good way is, And walk in it; Then you will find rest for your souls. But they said, 'We will not walk in it.'" (Jeremiah 6:16)

2. Should a believer divorce an unbelieving spouse?

A person might have been married as an unbeliever. If this person has now become a believer, is it appropriate to remain married to his or her spouse if the spouse is an unbeliever and has chosen not to become a believer? Paul addressed this issue in his letter to the Corinthians. A believer is not to divorce an unbelieving spouse as long as the spouse chooses to remain married to the believer.

"But to the rest I, not the Lord, say: If any brother has a wife who does not believe, and she is willing to live with him, let him not divorce her. And a woman who has a husband who does not believe, if he is willing to live with

> her, let her not divorce him. For the unbelieving husband is sanctified by the wife, and the unbelieving wife is sanctified by the husband; otherwise your children would be unclean, but now they are holy. But if the unbeliever departs, let him depart; a brother or a sister is not under bondage in such cases, But God has called us to peace. For how do you know, O wife, whether you will save your husband? Or how do you know, O husband, whether you will save your wife?" (I Corinthians 7:12-16)

3. Can a person remarry after divorce?

The New Testament discusses only two situations in which divorce is permissible. Remarriage is permissible (not commanded) when either of these situations occur and following the death of a spouse.

a. *Sexual immorality*

Jesus made it clear that marriage was intended for life and divorce was permitted only on grounds of marital unfaithfulness, i.e., sexual immorality. In such cases, remarriage is permissible. This assertion is captured in the following passage:

> "And I (Jesus) say to you, whoever divorces his wife, except for sexual immorality, and marries another, commits adultery; and whoever marries her who is divorced commits adultery." (Matthew 19:26; cf. Mark 10:11)

The apostle, Paul, also reminded the Corinthian believers that marriage was intended for life and divorce was against the will of God. If someone chooses to divorce a partner, outside those situations in which divorce is permissible, he or she is to remain unmarried:

> "Now to the married I command, yet not I but the Lord: A wife is not to depart from her husband. But even if she does depart, let her remain unmarried or be reconciled to her husband. And a husband is not to divorce his wife." (I Corinthians 7:10-11)

b. Departure of an unbelieving spouse

The covenant of marriage is no longer binding when an unbelieving spouse abandons a believing partner. In this case, the believer is not under obligation to remain single and may remarry, if desired.

> "And a woman who has a husband who does not believe, if he is willing to live with her, let her not divorce him. But if the unbeliever departs, let him depart; a brother or a sister is not under bondage in such cases." (I Corinthians 7:13, 15)

c. Death of a spouse

The marriage covenant is effective only as long as a couple lives, and remarriage is permissible following the death of a spouse. If a spouse dies, the living partner is released from the marriage covenant and has a choice to remain a widow(er) or remarry.

> "Or do you not know, brethren (for I speak to those who know the law), that the law has dominion over a man as long as he lives? For the woman who has a husband is bound by the law to her husband as long as he lives. But if the husband dies, she is released from the law of her husband. So then if, while her husband lives, she marries another man, she will be called an adulteress;

> but if her husband dies, she is free from that law, so that she is no adulteress, though she has married another man." (Romans 7:1-3)

> "A wife is bound by law as long as her husband lives; but if her husband dies, she is at liberty to be married to whom she wishes, only in the Lord (i.e., to a believer)." (I Corinthians 7:39)

There are many reasons for divorce in contemporary society. A discussion of individual divorce situations is outside the scope of this book and readers are encouraged to seek counseling from their local pastor or a Christian marriage counselor.

While it is true that God gives a second chance to those who genuinely repent of their sins, divorce is a traumatic experience and the scar may last a lifetime. Therefore, I encourage all those who know the Lord to please avoid divorce at all cost.

The Bible clearly teaches that every sin may be forgiven, except the sin of blasphemy against the Holy Spirit.

> "Therefore I say to you, every sin and blasphemy will be forgiven men, but the blasphemy against the Spirit will not be forgiven men. Anyone who speaks a word against the Son of Man, it will be forgiven him; but whoever speaks against the Holy Spirit, it will not be forgiven him, either in this age or in the age to come." (Matthew 12:31-32)

Divorce is not an unpardonable sin, but it is clearly not the will of God, hence must be discouraged. Divorce may lead to adultery which, in turn, is a sin against one's body.

> "Flee sexual immorality. Every sin that a man does is outside the body, but he who commits sexual immorality sins against his own body." (1 Corinthians 6:18)

The following passages should offer hope and encouragement to persons who have gone through or are going through divorce.

> "Come now, and let us reason together, says the Lord, though your sins are like scarlet, they shall be as white as snow; though they are red like crimson, they shall be as wool." (Isaiah 1:18)

> "Blessed is he whose transgression is forgiven, Whose sin is covered. Blessed is the man to whom the Lord does not impute iniquity, and in whose spirit there is no deceit." (Psalm 32:1-2)

> "The Lord is merciful and gracious, slow to anger, and abounding in mercy. He will not always strive with us, nor will He keep His anger forever. He has not dealt with us according to our iniquities. For as the heavens are high above the earth, so great is His mercy toward those who fear Him; As the east is from the west, so far has He removed our transgressions from us. As a father pities his children, so the Lord pities those who fear Him. For He knows our frame; He remembers that we are dust." (Psalm 103:8-14)

> "If You, Lord, should mark iniquities, O Lord, who could stand? But there is forgiveness with You, That You may be feared." (Psalm 130:3-4)

"He who believes in Him [Jesus Christ] is not condemned; but he who does not believe is condemned already, because he has not believed in the name of the only begotten Son of God." (John 3:18)

"There is therefore now no condemnation to those who are in Christ Jesus, who do not walk according to the flesh, but according to the Spirit. For the law of the Spirit of life in Christ Jesus has made me free from the law of sin and death. For what the law could not do in that it was weak through the flesh, God did by sending His own Son in the likeness of sinful flesh, on account of sin: He condemned sin in the flesh, that the righteous requirement of the law might be fulfilled in us who do not walk according to the flesh but according to the Spirit." (Romans 8:1-3)

"For Christ is the end of the law for righteousness to everyone who believes." (Romans 10:4)

"Therefore, if anyone is in Christ, he is a new creation; old things have passed away; behold, all things have become new." (II Corinthians 5:17)

"If we confess our sins, He [God] is faithful and just to forgive us our sins and to cleanse us from all unrighteousness." (I John 1:8)

SATAN

How sad that many Christians fail to realize that Satan is the number one enemy of the home. He knows the potential damage that two godly people who are in agreement can inflict upon his kingdom; therefore, he fights the relationship with all his might. First, he will do everything possible to prevent a couple from coming together in the first instance. If they successfully come together, he will next try to break up the relationship by any means possible. When Christians have conflicts in the home, they must see beyond the notion that the partner is the cause of the troubles in the home and realize that the devil is behind it all. God's Word warns:

> *"Be sober, be vigilant; because your adversary the devil walks about like a roaring lion, seeking whom he may devour."* (I Peter 5:8)

> *"The thief [devil] does not come except to steal, and to kill, and to destroy."* (John 10:10)

Anything that is potentially fatal or destructive comes from the devil. Since the devil is a spirit, the battles in our homes that manifest physically are actually of a spiritual origin. No one can fight spiritual battles with physical weapons. According to God's Word,

> *"We do not wrestle against flesh and blood, but against principalities, against powers, against the rulers of the darkness of this age, against spiritual hosts of wickedness in the heavenly places."* (Ephesians 6:12)

Therefore, we are further reminded that,

> *"The weapons of our warfare are not carnal but mighty in God for pulling down strongholds, casting down arguments and every high thing that exalts itself against the knowledge of God, bringing every thought into captivity to the obedience of Christ."* (II Corinthians 10:4-5)

To fight spiritual battles, believers are told to

> *"Be strong in the Lord and in the power of His might. Put on the whole armor of God that you may be able to stand against the wiles of the devil"* (Ephesians 6:10-11)

> *"Therefore take up the whole armor of God, that you may be able to withstand in the evil day, and having done all, to stand. Stand therefore, having girded your waist with truth, having put on the breastplate of righteousness, and having shod your feet with the preparation of the gospel of peace; above all, taking the shield of faith with which you will be able to quench all the fiery darts of the wicked one. And take the helmet of salvation, and the sword of the Spirit, which is the word of God; praying always with all prayer and supplication in the Spirit, being watchful to this end with all perseverance and supplication for all the saints"* (Ephesians 6:13-18)

An Unforgiving Spirit

Forgiveness is necessary for the success of any relationship since offenses are bound to arise. God's word on forgiveness is quite clear.

> *"For if you forgive men their trespasses, your heavenly Father will also forgive you. But if you do not forgive men their trespasses, neither will your Father forgive your trespasses."* (Matthew 6:14-15)

> *"Let all bitterness, wrath, anger, clamor, and evil speaking be put away from you, with all malice. And be kind to one another, tenderhearted, forgiving one another, even as God in Christ forgave you."* (Ephesians 4:31-32)

Peter asked the Lord how many times a person ought to forgive another. Jesus replied,

> "*I do not say to you, up to seven times, but up to seventy times seven.*" (Matthew 18:22)

Nowhere is forgiveness needed more often than in marriage. A good principle to apply whenever there is a misunderstanding is what I call the twelve-hour rule. Since the period from the rising of the sun to its going down is approximately twelve hours, it is good advice to resolve lingering issues within twelve hours.

> "*Be angry, and do not sin: do not let the sun go down on your wrath, nor give place to the devil.*" (Ephesians 4:26-27)

Sometimes, it may not be possible to resolve a problem within this twelve-hour time frame, but attempts must be made to resolve issues at the earliest possible opportunity. The longer ill-feelings are harbored, the more difficult it becomes to resolve them. If a family cultivates the habit of a family devotion, then this principle can be applied easily since it will be difficult to approach the throne of God with unresolved issues in our hearts.

TELEVISION

Television has brought us a mixed baggage of good and evil. We are able to visualize events as they happen and even view archived documents through a video attached to the television. However, television has now taken over the lives of many people, with potentially disastrous consequences for the family. Some parents have completely abandoned the care of their children to the television. Rather than spending quality time with their children, they simply turn them over to the television as a means of diverting their attention from parental care. This is an ugly situation. Too many programs on television are not suitable for children, yet they are given total liberty to watch such programs. To make matters worse, many homes now feature television in the children's rooms, thus giving them unrestricted access to any program of their choice. As might be expected, it is easier to cultivate a greater attraction for programs that are unhealthy than for programs that edify spiritually. Children will naturally prefer to watch programs that are full of violence or immorality over programs that teach good moral values. Some husbands have no time for their wives because they have to watch sports on television. Likewise, many wives watch soap operas rather than give attention to their husbands, children or household chores. Christians must learn to draw the line on how much television they as parents, or their children, watch. It is shameful for a family to break up simply because of this uncontrolled appetite.

Friends, Relations, and Other people

The easiest way to introduce problems into your home is to allow others to intrude into personal matters. Discussing your family affairs with parents, siblings, in-laws, friends, co-workers, and others simply exposes you and your family to unsolicited advice that may break up your home. If a man cannot make decisions for his family unless he first consults with his father or mother, then he is not yet ready to start a home. Such a man is indeed a boy, not a man, and no boy should go into marriage. God expects a man to

> "...leave his father and mother and be joined to his wife, and the two shall become one flesh." (Matthew 19:5)

Likewise, a woman who takes her family secrets to her mother and friends is inviting trouble into her home. Not all friends are happy when a marriage is successful, particularly when theirs is unsuccessful. Thus, everyone must watch what they say to other people about their spouse or children. Couples must seek every possible means to work through their problems themselves. When this is unsuccessful, their next step should be to talk to their pastor. Beware of the advice you get from other people, and remember,

> *"Blessed is the man Who walks not in the counsel of the ungodly, Nor stands in the path of sinners, Nor sits in the seat of the scornful; But his delight is in the law of the Lord, and in His law he meditates day and night. He shall be like a tree planted by the rivers of water, that brings forth its fruit in its season, whose leaf also shall not wither; and whatsoever he does shall prosper."*
> (Psalm 1:1-3)

The principle here is to seek help as soon as you realize that your marriage is beginning to exhibit signs of a crack in the relationship. Once there is a crack, it must either be mended or it will get worse. It can never get better if nothing is done. Cracks in marriages are like tears in our clothes. If not mended, tears only get worse never better.

Dishonesty

A strong marriage is founded upon the principle of honesty. Deception is a sure recipe for marital failure. No matter what a spouse has done, honesty will help in the healing process. Dishonesty, on the other hand, will lead to suspicion, lack of satisfaction, and a deepening sense of hurt and betrayal.

> "Therefore, putting away lying, let each one of you speak truth with his neighbor, for we are members of one another." (Ephesians 4:25)

FINANCES

As important as money may seem, the following anonymous sayings are truly thought-provoking:

- Money can buy a house, but not a home.
- Money can buy a bed, but not sleep.
- Money can buy a clock, but not time.
- Money can buy a book, but not knowledge.
- Money can buy food, but not an appetite.
- Money can buy position, but not respect.
- Money can buy blood, but not life.
- Money can buy medicine, but not health.
- Money can buy sex, but not love.
- Money can buy insurance, but not safety.
- Money can buy…but not…

I call money the "monster of the home." Sadly enough, money is the root of many of the problems husbands and wives face. If a couple can overpower this monster, they are more likely to have a happy marriage, since they will have overcome the single most common cause of tension in the home. The Word of God sends a clear message on the problems associated with money:

> "Now godliness with contentment is great gain. For we brought nothing into this world, and it is certain we can carry nothing out. And having food and clothing, with these we shall be content. But those who desire to be rich

fall into temptation and a snare, and into many foolish and harmful lusts which drown men in destruction and perdition. For the love of money is a root of all kinds of evil, for which some have strayed from the faith in their greediness, and pierced themselves through with many sorrows." (1 Timothy 6:6-10)

"But woe to you who are rich, For you have received your consolation." (Luke 6:24)

Money is not bad in its own right, but the love of it is iniquitous. We all need money to survive in a money-loving, money-worshiping world. However, Christians are encouraged to depend on God for all of their needs. He has promised:

"The young lions lack and suffer hunger; but those who seek the Lord shall not lack any good thing." (Psalm 34:10)

"I have been young, and now am old; yet I have not seen the righteous forsaken, nor his descendants begging bread." (Psalm 37:25)

"And my God shall supply all your need according to His riches in glory by Christ Jesus." (Philippians 4:19)

Christians are not to love the world and the things that are in it—including money!

"Do not love the world or the things in the world. If anyone loves the world, the love of the Father is not in him. For all that is in the world—the lust of the flesh, the lust of the eyes, and the pride of live—is not of the Father but

is of the world. And the world is passing away, and the lust of it; but he who does the will of God abides forever." (1 John 2:15-17)

God has promised to provide for our needs if He is preeminent in our lives.

"But seek first the kingdom of God and His righteousness, and all these things shall be added to you." (Matthew 6:33)

God cares for us.

"Casting all your cares upon Him, for He cares for you." (I Peter 5:7)

We are also warned about the dangers of accumulating wealth on earth:

"Do not lay up for yourselves treasures on earth, where moth and rust destroy and where thieves break in and steal; but lay up for yourselves treasures in heaven, where neither moth nor rust destroys and where thieves do not break in and steal. For where your treasure is, there your heart will be also." (Matthew 6:19-21)

Furthermore,

"If then you were raised with Christ, seek those things which are above, where Christ is, sitting at the right hand of God. Set your mind on things above, not on things on the earth." (Colossians 3:1-2)

Some Christians develop so much love for money that they have literally abandoned the faith of our Lord Jesus Christ in order to pursue this monster without hindrance. We always ought to remember that we brought nothing into this world and will leave with nothing.

> "For we brought nothing into this world, and it is certain we can carry nothing out." (I Timothy 6:7)

For the love of money, many people have abandoned their spouses and family for years and they have been separated by countries, states or cities, with no viable plans for reuniting. Through such a protracted separation, the devil is given room to invade the family. Problems of sexual immorality, lack of parental guidance for children, and similar problems of great magnitude may arise. In the worst cases, some marriages have ended in divorce. It is not worth abandoning one's family for an unnecessarily protracted length of time simply in the pursuit of money.

There are instances when temporary separations are inevitable. For example, a person may be on a military or missionary assignment in which it is not possible for the family to go. Other instances include a job-related transfer, enrollment in school, etc. Even in these cases, an effort should be made to maintain close ties with family members through telephone calls, mail, and frequent visits. The basic principle is that a person ought not to abandon his or her family for any period of time longer than necessary.

Problems about money often arise in the way the money is spent. One partner may be a wasteful spender whereas the other is not; one may be generous, the other a miser; one may be modest, the other fashion-conscious; one may be the sole breadwinner, the other may contribute nothing to the family financially. These differences often create problems. For example, the sole bread-winner might assume he or she is entitled to more of the family's resources than the spouse who is not bringing money into the family. That might seem reasonable, but it is wrong and unrealistic.

Every couple ought to know that a family has only one "purse" and all income of any member of the family belongs in that purse. It belongs to the entire family, not just the one who brings in the income. There should be no individual ownership. In spending family resources, however, every member of the family must be considerate of the other members. Selfishness and greed must be avoided. There are wives who want to always be clothed in beautiful dresses, with no regard for what their husbands or children wear. The converse may be true. This is one reason that couples may not want to keep a joint account. In either case, this is selfish and ungodly.

Furthermore, family finances must not be spent extravagantly. It is a good practice for a couple to maintain a joint account. In doing so, they need to agree on what amount the partner is allowed to spend at will without consultation with or prior approval of the spouse. It is a good practice to agree together on major projects such as buying a new car, a home, furniture, etc. In keeping a joint account, couples must be honest and unselfish. Whenever possible, the interest of the entire family must come before the interest of an individual member of the family. We must always resist the temptation of allowing money to become a source of conflict in the home.

Whenever major problems arise in the family on account of finances, it signals the need for a couple to seek counseling from a Christian financial counselor or another believer.

Career

Some people's careers are more important to them than their families. Consequently, they abandon their families in pursuit of these careers. Some are engaged in private business and they place the business over the family. Such an attitude can lead to serious problems in the home. What a spouse or children needs is not money deposited in the family's account, but love and warmth. Thus, a family might enjoy a fat bank account or other investments, yet lack happiness and fellowship in the home.

As important as our careers may seem, the family is more important. Some careers require us to be away from home or spend long hours away from home, yet quality time must be created in the midst of those tight schedules to express the warmth and love the family needs. In certain instances, some couples may not see each other for five to six days every week because they have planned their dual work schedules to cover all of the twenty-four hours in a day. The plan is such that as one spouse is returning to the house from work, the other is leaving. Money is not the "be-all-and-end-all" of life and does not necessarily bring happiness. Time must be created for fun and family adventures. Our joy as Christians must not come from money but from the Lord, the ultimate source of true and lasting joy. Remember,

"...*the joy of the Lord is your strength.*" (Nehemiah 8:10)

Lack of, or Ineffective, Communication

In some homes there is hardly any communication. Some wives are afraid to express their thoughts to their husbands. Likewise, some wives are so garrulous, their husbands may not have a chance to open a discussion. Communication is a two-way process in which one person conveys a message and the other listens. In addition, communication must ensure that there is room for the listener to respond to the message. If this is lacking, then communication becomes a one-way process and leads to frustration. Moderation should be the key.

If a member of the family has a problem that needs to be discussed, there ought to be avenues for such discussions. This means time must be set aside. How can a wife express her feelings to her husband if he is never at home, and vice versa? If a spouse cannot express his or her feelings to the partner, this often encourages discussing such feelings with other people such as friends and parents. As discussed earlier, this may generate problems in the home.

Each member of a couple ought to be both a good listener and a good communicator. No matter how silly a spouse might think his or her partner's concerns are, attempts must be made to address the concerns with a view to providing lasting solutions. Such concerns may simply be the tip of an iceberg of a more serious underlying problem, and failure to address them early may lead to undesirable consequences. Open communication must be maintained between a couple, and problems must not be allowed to linger for too long without serious attempts to address and solve them. Help should be sought when a couple cannot resolve a serious problem by themselves. Communication is vital to the success and survival of any relationship.

COMPUTERS

Computers come with much potential for doing great things and getting important tasks accomplished. Yet, they also come with a baggage of problems. With the advent of the internet, there is much out there to occupy a person's time and one must exercise discipline. A person may become addicted to computers the same way he or she may be addicted to television or other habits. One must not allow the computer to rule one's life and family. Anything that controls a person is that person's master.

> *"Do you not know that to whom you present yourselves slaves to obey, you are that one's slaves whom you obey, whether of sin leading to death, or of obedience leading to righteousness?"* (Romans 6:16)

A Christian must not be in bondage to anything. We have been set free by our Lord Jesus Christ and must remain free.

Quarrels

Misunderstandings are bound to come when two people live together. Disagreements may come because of individual preferences but these must not be allowed to take over our lives. We must be sensitive to each other's needs, placing our spouse's interests and needs above ours. We should honestly seek to resolve problems at the very earliest opportunity instead of allowing them to linger.

> *"Therefore, putting away lying, 'Let each one of you speak truth with his neighbor,' for we are members of one another. Be angry, and do not sin: do not let the sun go down on your wrath, nor give place to the devil. Let him who stole steal no longer, but rather let him labor, working with his hands what is good, that he may have something to give him who has need. Let no corrupt word*

proceed out of your mouth, but what is good for necessary edification, that it may impart grace to the hearers. And do not grieve the Holy Spirit of God, by whom you were sealed for the day of redemption. Let all bitterness, wrath, anger, clamor, and evil speaking be put away from you, with all malice. And be kind to one another, tenderhearted, forgiving one another even as God in Christ forgave you." (Ephesians 4:25-32)

"Husbands, likewise, dwell with them with understanding, giving honor to the wife, as to the weaker vessel, and as being heirs together of the grace of life, that your prayers may not be hindered." (I Peter 3:7)

"Even so the tongue is a little member and boasts great things. See how great a forest a little fire kindles! And the tongue is a fire, a world of iniquity. The tongue is so set among our members that it defiles the whole body, and sets on fire the course of nature; and it is set on fire by hell. For every kind of beast and bird, of reptile and creature of the sea, is tamed and has been tamed by mankind. But no man can tame the tongue. It is an unruly evil, full of deadly poison. With it we bless our God and Father, and with it we curse men, who have been made in the similitute of God. Out of the same mouth proceed blessing and cursing. My brethren, these things ought not to be so. Does a spring send forth fresh water and bitter from the same opening? Can a fig tree, my brethren, bear olives, or a grapevine bear figs? Thus no spring yields both salt water and fresh. Who is wise and understanding among you? Let him show by good conduct that his works are done in the meekness of wisdom. But if you have bitter envy and

self-seeking in your hearts, do not boast and lie against the truth. This wisdom does not descend from above, but is earthly, sensual, demonic. For where envy and self-seeking exist, confusion and every evil thing are there. But the wisdom that is from above is first pure, then peaceable, gentle, willing to yield, full of mercy and good fruits, without partiality and without hypocrisy. Now the fruit of righteousness is sown in peace by those who make peace."
(James 3:5-18)

SUMMARY

The following conditions or persons may threaten or break up a happy marriage relationship: adultery, bigamy or polygamy, divorce, Satan, an unforgiving spirit, television, computer, friends and relations, dishonesty, finances, career, quarrels, and the lack of communication.

CHALLENGES

1. Are you happy with the present state of your marriage?
2. Can you identify specific factors that are threatening your marriage?
3. Are you willing to make necessary adjustments to improve your relationship with your spouse? What are these adjustments?

11

Additional Family Issues

Family Devotions

It is often said that a family that prays together, stays together. The importance of family devotions cannot be overemphasized. Members of a family are drawn together when they come in unity into the presence of the Lord. It is extremely difficult to approach God while harboring grudges against a member of the family. We would feel a sense of hypocrisy if we were to approach God knowing we have something against someone with whom we are praying. Thus, devotions create an opportunity for resolving problems before they get out of hand.

During family devotions, members of the family have a chance to learn about God and to take their problems to Him. Family crises are more likely to escalate and less likely to be resolved quickly in homes lacking family devotions than those having devotions. During family devotions, children have the opportunity to learn from their parents how to pray. Many of the problems that surface in the family can generally be more easily resolved if a family prays together. Family devotions ought to be a standard practice in any Christian home.

Family Planning

A couple needs to discuss various family planning options with their healthcare provider. (It is better if this is done before marriage.) Both partners must be in agreement as to what option is best for them.

Cross-Cultural Marriage

A cross-cultural marriage is a marriage involving spouses of different cultural backgrounds, such as persons of a different ethnic group, race or nationality. These marriages present a unique problem. For such a marriage to be successful, both partners must take time to understand each other's beliefs and customs and be committed to allowing God's culture, which transcends any earthly culture, to be the dominant culture of the home. To ignore that cultural differences present a potential ground for misunderstandings, and assume that all is well, is to live in self-deception.

Over time, the devil will use any cultural difference as an opportunity to invade a marriage and create unnecessary pain for a couple or family. A couple must resolve any concerns about cultural differences during courtship, before they say, "I

Additional Family Issues

do." Cultural differences are not insurmountable for a Christian couple, but they need to be recognized and dealt with appropriately.

Sex in marriage

Sex is not dirty as some consider it. Sex was made by God as a perfect gift, not only to human beings but also to other animals. Human beings have perverted sex, thereby making it look like something evil. The best way to enjoy sex is within the context of marriage, as it is the only context in which it can be experienced without guilt. Sex carried out in any other way will be fraught with guilt and emptiness, rather than the satisfaction God intended it to bring. Sex has been used for reasons totally unintended by God. Some women use it as an object of punishment for their husbands. When a husband fails to do what his wife wants, she may deprive him of sex. This is wrong for a Christian woman to do. It is equally wrong for a Christian husband to deprive his wife of sex for any reason. Sexual deprivation must always be by consent of both partners, specifically when they decide to give themselves to prayer and fasting. Sex, when carried out according to God's instructions, can add considerable enjoyment to a marriage.

> *"Now concerning the things of which you wrote to me: It is good for a man not to touch a woman. Nevertheless, because of sexual immorality, let each man have his own wife, and let each woman have her own husband. Let the husband render to his wife the affection due her, and likewise also the wife to her husband. The wife does not have authority over his own body, but the husband does. And likewise the husband does not have authority over his*

own body, but the wife does. Do not deprive one another except with consent for a time, that you may give yourselves to fasting and prayer; and come together again so that Satan does not tempt you because of your lack of self-control." (1 Corinthians 7:1-5)

DRIVING TO CHURCH TOGETHER

Some couples have the practice of going to church in separate vehicles even if one vehicle can accommodate the entire family. Unless it cannot be helped, such as in the rare instances when a partner has an early function in the church or another genuine reason, it is advisable that a family drive to church together in the same vehicle. This fosters unity within the family.

GODLINESS

After all is said and done, godliness is the key to achieving a solid and lasting marital relationship. If a family crowns God as the Head of the home, then every member of the family will be subject to Him and no one will be self-seeking, but rather submissive to Him and to one another in love. Without God, it is extremely difficult, if not impossible, for a strong family relationship to exist. He is the author of marriage and ought to be given first place in a Christian family. As much as a couple strives to please each other, pleasing God must always take preeminence. When a person pleases the Lord, it becomes easy to please a partner. God ought to be so prominent in Christian homes that these homes become a role model for the world. As a couple builds their home together, let them remember the following words of our Lord Jesus Christ:

Additional Family Issues

"You are the salt of the earth; but if the salt loses its flavor, how shall it be seasoned? It is then good for nothing but to be thrown out and trampled underfoot by men. You are the light of the world. A city that is set on a hill cannot be hidden. Nor do they light a lamp and put it under a basket, but on a lamp-stand, and it gives light to all who are in the house. Let your light so shine before men, that they may see your good works and glorify your Father in heaven." (Matthew 5:13-16)

Summary

1. Family devotions need to be an integral part of a Christian family.
2. Godliness is key to a successful Christian marriage.
3. The method of family planning adopted by a couple needs to be chosen by mutual consent.
4. Sexual intercourse, carried out within the bounds of marriage, can spice up a marriage.
5. It is good for a couple or family to drive to church in the same vehicle, if space and time permit.
6. When persons of different cultures desire to marry, they must resolve any concerns about their different cultural backgrounds prior to saying "I do."

Challenges

1. Do you currently hold family devotions? If you do not, will you commit to starting them?
2. Are you married to or proposing to be married to someone of a different culture? What steps will you take to resolve any issues related to your cultural differences?

About the Author

Jethro Ekuta was born and raised in Nigeria. His parents, Samson and Florence, both believers, brought him up "in the way that he should go." He accepted Jesus Christ as his personal Lord and Savior in 1976, while in high school. Having earned the Doctor of Veterinary Medicine (D.V.M.) degree, he worked as a lecturer at Ahmadu Bello University and as a research scientist at the National Institute for Pharmaceutical Research and Development in Nigeria before immigrating to the United States in 1990.

Jethro earned the Doctor of Philosophy (Ph.D.) degree in Pharmacology and Toxicology from the University of Mississippi. He undertook postdoctoral training in cardiovascular pharmacology at Meharry Medical College in Nashville, Tennessee, sponsored by the National Heart, Lung, and Blood Institute of the National Institutes of Health (N.I.H.). He subsequently received training in clinical pharmacology through a fellowship sponsored by the United States Food and Drug Administration (F.D.A.). He currently works for a pharmaceutical company based in Cincinnati, Ohio.

Jethro has been active in various capacities in the local churches where he has been a member. He has served as a Sunday school teacher, preacher, home fellowship leader, church secretary, and member of the church council. He currently fellowships at Faith Bible Church, Cincinnati, Ohio.

Jethro is happily married to Roseline. The couple is blessed with four children—Victor, Joy, Peace, and Patience.

Marriage—
As God Intended It to Be!
Order Form

Postal orders: Dr. Jethro Ekuta
7733 Albright Court
Mason, OH 45040

Telephone orders: (513) 754-1351

Please send *Marriage—As God Intended It to Be!* **to:**

Name: _____

Address: _____

City: _____ State: _____

Zip: _____

Telephone: (_____) _____

Book Price: $12.95

Shipping: $3.00 for the first book and $1.00 for each additional book to cover shipping and handling within US, Canada, and Mexico. International orders add $6.00 for the first book and $2.00 for each additional book

Or order from:
ACW Press
5501 N. 7th. Ave. #502
Phoenix, AZ 85013

(800) 931-BOOK

or contact your local bookstore